JACOB'S LADDER

BECOMING THE CHANGE I WANTED TO SEE

JACOB BRAMLETT

JACOB'S LADDER

BECOMING THE CHANGE I WANTED TO SEE

Published by Krystal Lee Enterprises (KLE Publishing)
Please send comments and questions:

Krystal Lee Enterprises
770-240-0089 Ext. 1
sales@KLEPub.com

To Reach the Author:
Email: jbramlett97@gmail.com
TikTok: IsDatJacob @isdatjacob_10

Cover Design: Jacob Bramlett

ISBN: **979-8-89987-911-1**

dedication

This book is dedicated to my Lord and Savior, Jesus Christ. The one that rose from the dead. The one that is still living. The one who heals sickness and continues to heal. The one that defeated death. The perfect one. Jesus overcame the world and death.

Thank you, Lord, for what You have done on Calvary. I just want you to be proud of me. Fill me with your ways so I can be selfless. Convict me from my thoughts and from things that are not like you, Lord. Protect the path I am on and do not let me quit for nothing. I am holding you accountable to your word, Lord.

JACOB'S LADDER

BECOMING THE CHANGE I WANTED TO SEE

Table of Contents

introduction

Jacob's Ladder

Dear younger me, you didn't know many things. You didn't know how life would turn out or why certain things were going to happen to you. And that's ok. You were just young and trying to make sense of a world that often didn't make sense. You made choices based on what you understood then, not what you know now. You were not supposed to have it all figured out.

You responded to pain, confusion, and pressure the only way you knew how: by surviving. And that in and of itself was an act of strength. You didn't fail. You were growing through things you didn't even have words to convey. I see that now, and I honor you for every moment you kept going, even when it felt like no one noticed how hard it was.

There was never anything wrong with you. You were not too much, not too sensitive, and not broken. You were learning how to carry emotions that no one taught you how to hold. You were doing the best you could. And I'm proud of you.

You are loved, not just now, but back then, when you felt unseen or misunderstood. You are still learning and still healing. There is always something good in you. There was always something special about you, from then and even until now.

You do not have to harm yourself for God to come save you and love you. So stop cutting yourself. Stop beating yourself up all the time. Keep living and become the change you want to see in this world. You are truly loved by God and destined for greatness. Don't ever think you could have changed someone.

The people who always wanted you to be dead really meant it by how they treated you and what was told to you. But, you should not have gotten comfortable with people cursing you, beating you, and downing you as a child. The parent who told you you should not exist should know that someday you will tell your story, and that day is today.

Do not die on me. What if you did not exist today? What will the world be missing? Without God, there will be no Jacob. I just wanna go back and hug you, Lil J, so bad. You have gone through and experienced so much. Even though you felt you were walking through this life alone, I am so proud of you. Keep going and keep the faith in the Lord Jesus Christ! He has risen and loves you for who you are. Jesus is alive.

Sincerely,

Love Jacob, from your older self.

JACOB'S LADDER

BECOMING THE CHANGE I WANTED TO SEE

chapter

one

Redemption

EPHESIANS 1:7-8

"Christ sacrificed his life's blood to set us free, which means our sins are now forgiven. Christ did this because of God's gift of undeserved grace to us. God has great wisdom and understanding."

Redemption can sometimes be a painful process. Growing up I had to live through so much, and some of it impacted the type of adult I would become. I cannot say that it broke me, because I have accomplished so much. I want to show you how God took the child I was, and made me the man I wanted to see. The title of this book, *Be the Change You Want to See*, is about becoming the person you were born to be and the child in you need to see.

How could I have ever known I would be in

management at a large global chain. To date, I have worked in management for six years. I was the child many ignored, so it is ironic I am now managing a lot of people most of which are minors. Today, I drive a BMW. I never would have guessed I would get blessed with a black man's wish, or a "BMW".

I never thought I would get my license because when I asked for help, too many turned me away. Even at the drivers bureau I got a story to tell. I overcame everything I faced while being homeless for a period of time. When I didn't know my way out, I think, *How can it be possible I have lived through so much and accomplished so much so young in my life?*

I can say, it's possible when you keep the faith and keep pressing forward. There should never be a moment when you allow yourself to lose your faith or hope. I had to always remember to keep the faith in the Lord Jesus Christ and always push forward. The path God has you on, trust Him to bring you through because "All things are possible" (Matthew 19:26). "Never look back, Jacob," is what I started to tell myself. "The past is dead and gone. So don't rebirth it. Leave the past in the grave where it belongs."

I truly thank God for the blessings, lessons, the betrayal, etc. The list really goes on, but it is not all that important. All of it strengthened me into the man God called me to be. The crazy part about it, there are plenty of people asking me questions I never expected to hear. I've been asked, "Are you perfect, Jacob?"

Well, there is only one person who is perfect. I can tell you that the only person who walked this earth who was perfect was, "Jesus". He is the only individual who walked on this earth who never sinned. That's why we look up to Him because he is a perfect example of who we want to be like.

I can look back over my life and say, "Look at God." The conversations I had with God, He answered them in his timing. "He will never come when we want him to, but he will come right on time" is a favorite quote and song I know. God knows all. He's omniscient. I am not perfect, I just believe that what I was asking God for, he would do it for me if it was his will.

Jesus stated, "**If you ask me for anything in my name, I will do it**" (John 14:14). I feel like the things we want for are because we have not asked for them sincerely. Have you heard of this line, "A closed mouth doesn't get fed?" So you can get my point.

If we don't have the things we need or want, and we have not asked God, we cannot complain that we are starving. We have to put God in a position to bless us by not asking "amiss". All that to say, "Don't be scared to ask God for anything." He wants to hear from us. He loves to listen to our voices and you should know that our voices matter to God.

I wish I could talk to my younger self because I want to tell me then how God is always good. God is good even when we face trials and tribulations. I had to release pain to see who

I truly was called to be and that wasn't easy. I read this book from author K Lee, "Release Pain: From Bondage to Freedom," and it helped me tremendously to uncover many things I didn't know about my emotional growth journey.

Release Pain

AuthorKLee.com

I would encourage anyone to get that book and pair it with mine to see how you too may need to speak and help heal the younger you buried within. It took me getting older to realize I had the power through Christ to release pain. "Don't hold the pain in," I had to tell my younger self. "Release the pain you've been holding inside."

I'm telling you that this book will bless your life to help you open up about thoughts and pain points that keep you in bondage. This book encouraged me greatly to tell my story and release the pain I felt, but not so I can leak pain on others. I wanted to write this book to share my growth story and the miracles that have happened that make me a marvel.

I grew up with trials and tribulations. People

doubted what I would become or if I would make it. I never let that stop me from achieving.

Fast forwarding a bit, today. I am a manger who has had to learn and battle to get where I am. The real me is a black man, young, educated, and some would argue I have documented challenges.

I don't see my medical history as a means for people to doubt what I can do. I have always been a go-getter and wanted to do things for myself. In part, because I got tired of waiting and relying on people to do things for me. I needed to embrace my own power.

On the job, I had to deal with racial discrimination, harassment, and retaliation. Yes, you read it right. I remember thinking when some of the managers talked to me, some of whom have the same title and less experience than me like, "We are not in the 1600s anymore. I am free." I didn't like not being heard or dismissed as if what I am saying doesn't matter. This pattern of communication and dismissal, I noticed, was an old problem, tied to a deep rooted pain from my childhood.

It was only a matter of time before I would learn to defend myself and appear to be the angry black man no one wanted to see. Slavery began in 1619, in Jamestown, Virginia. It's funny that we are in the year 2025 and a grown man can be called a boy. I get that I am a young man, but I am still a man. Sometimes I feel like my glasses can make people think I am a child. But as I work, and I do less talking and produce results instead, I start to realize the power that was hidden in my DNA over 400 years ago.

I am not saying that I always get it right. That I might not have acted a bit out of turn, but it was never in a way that deserved a disciplinary action. I remember speaking up for myself a few times after reading the book Embrace Your Crown: Open 7 Gates to Find and Overcome Heartbreak. Krystal (author K Lee) would encourage me to find my voice, and it was tricky at first because I was used to embracing what people wanted me to have. To be heard was different. So when a manager told me something and I simply said, "No. I cannot do that." They said I was insubordinate and deserved a disciplinary action.

Embrace Your Crown

EmbraceYourCrown.com

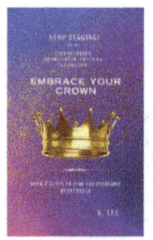

This wasn't the first time, in a few months time, as I learned to use my voice to speak up for myself, I got six write ups. The funny thing is, if you get more than a certain amount, the company/location would fire you. I was nearing that mark, but as they reviewed the notes of the complaint and my evidence, the disciplinary write ups were silently removed. This was one of the best victories I experienced up to this point in my life for giving me my voice.

I don't know if I was ever as bold as I am now, and I feel even as I write this book, my voice is growing stronger within me. I know I have the power to change my life and I am on a course to do that, to becoming the change I wanted to see. I was told that managerial misconduct was why the disciplinary actions were removed from my record but that wasn't what I could easily read on paper. Winning this battle at the onset didn't make things easier at work. I wasn't more appreciated, but was sidelined and undermined repeatedly.

I know you might say, why would you still endure this and not just quit, but hold that thought and I will explain. On my shift, I have requested assistance from workers who were under me with tasks that were in their job description and needed to be done each day. Workers I requested assistance from would be deliberately reassigned to other tasks by managers who felt their word superseded mine.

There were so many instances where they had me isolated and working alone it wasn't funny. The decisions they made appear retaliatory and undermines the support needed to complete my job effectively. I felt unsafe, unvalued, racially targeted, harassed, and unfairly disciplined.

It was clear that racial dynamics play a significant role in the way I was treated by management. I have faced harsher disciplinary actions compared to my white counterparts, who are often given more leniency or are allowed to bypass store policies. The management influence over store operations during their tenure and after to protect their favorite employees, particularly white men and female managers, has created an atmosphere where racial bias is not only tolerated but preferred.

I have repeatedly been disciplined for tasks I could not complete due to systemic issues within the workplace. I was reprimanded for my work or lack of management with no real means to get it done. Although I had received conflicting instructions from multiple managers and received no adequate support to complete my tasks, I was a celebrated employee who adds value.

Throughout the whole process, I was counting the long 4 years of working under a hostile work environment as "joy" (James 1:2). To your question, I couldn't quit because I would be quitting on the younger me. I had to grow through adversity and not cave into it. Stopping this journey would not pave away for someone else, not writing this book wasn't an option, after I knew what I needed to do.

I am writing this book for people who suffered discrimination not just because of race or age, but also for learning challenges. Although my medical history has challenges, I do not allow it to be a crutch. I know it is the law to provide reasonable accommodations to those with challenges to perform their jobs, but I can tell you I never got this treatment. I used to feel slighted by it, but then I saw how much it empowered me to transcend any of my challenges.

What I learned and want to share with you, you don't have to be perfect for people to think highly of you. You can have challenges where you are at and be in the right place. You can be doing what is right, and a fight still comes to your doorstep. We need Dr. Martin Luther King Jr back so we can protest and get stirred up about helping each other, I think sometimes. Then I realize, we bring back his dream when we connect and be the hands and feet to what he fought and was willing to give his life for.

Dr. King wasn't just for people who look like me, he was for the people. He realized our ability to embrace our unique differences was important for all of humanity. A discrimination or hatred problem with a section of us, will swell to a problem for all of us. He said this about America, "[America] struggle[s] for genuine equality on all levels. And this will be a much more difficult struggle."

We have to trust God in our process to redeem our time and value. Some people will misuse us and even attempt to abuse us. This is their choice, but I also have a choice. I had to realize my power and learn to say "yes" and "no" when I wanted.

This power, through the support of Christ, set me on a path of redemption. And I want to warn you, although the weapon is formed, no weapon formed against you shall prosper. We must trust God throughout our process.

I can say that I am the only one in my family

who's educated, and the only one who graduated from high school, got some college education, and is doing well in life. I was the first male in my family to receive my diploma. My parents and plenty of my elders never graduated as I was told. I had to break the generational curse over our blood line.

I did it for my siblings as well, since they never had an education and will never have an education by the hands of their own parents. I set an example to show others how to navigate life. God only knows people's paths in life, and I personally don't have a clue. All I can do is pray for others and God's direction for them every step of the way.

I didn't have someone to look up to while I was going through my seasons of hard changes. I looked up to God because He was the one who got me through. It was a season in my life when I was 20, and I only talked to God when my life was going good. When things hit rock bottom, I would abandon God.

Yes, I have abandoned God when things in my life were going left. I learned a good lesson on that, that I intend to share in this book. But I want to be clear, there are people who only talk to God when they need something. I wasn't that type of individual.

I owe God my life so I couldn't treat him like that. If I am honest, though, I did put him on the backburner when I felt like things weren't working. The position I am in, in my life right now, is all praise to the Father. He was the only thing consistent in my life, and going through the pain of being alone wasn't easy.

I didn't have a support system to go to. No parent or relative to lean on for support or advice. I just had God who gave me the consistent love I needed and I didn't recognize that fully until I was in my 20's. I struggled with feeling loved by my family and so called friends.

I am going to get into it, but I love how people ask me til this day, "How did you get the things you have?" or "Why are you always smiling and happy when I see you? There are people who will pray for your downfall, run your name through the mud, who will count you out, and plot against you. I love it when people get mad and bring up my past struggles.

I know I am not supposed to get mad, and I don't now, but I used to. I was down in this lifetime and lost many things constantly. I will never deny that the root of my pain was unknown. I had to learn how to be happy and the keys to stay happy.

Be Happy

AuthorKLee.com

Let's talk about the strength that I had to get up and get myself out of every situation without letting it defeat me. You want to know what is very interesting. Those same people who down you, can later on in life need you in some way that only God knows. But I have found that God will have you minister to and/or help people that have broken or betrayed you.

Today, there are people who have done that for me. People who I consider family who look out for me now. Dr. K Lee (Krystal) and her tribe are part of my family. Together, we set out on a path to help others, and in January 2025, we launched the book club called the "Growing Book Club."

This was an answer to a prayer I had prayed back in August 2024. It's amazing how God answers prayers; even the prayers that you forget about. I am still praying for the growth of the Growing Book Club because I see how much it has helped me since we started.

I don't know why there are so many jealous spirits around who want to see your downfall. I am not sure what the reason could be for why people don't want to be happy for the next individual? Life is too short to be praying for someone's downfall. Life should be all about surviving, loving God (because God is not dead), and enjoying life.

Buddha died. Muhammad died. They are both still in the grave. Jesus is alive, the Word is alive because He is risen. We celebrate as Christians because the Word that created everything with God, wants to be a joint heir with us.

He will be with us and will never forsake us no matter how hard it gets. He wanted his cup to pass from his lips but prayed the will of God over his circumstance. We too have to learn to pray for the will of God, no matter our test or situation.

JACOB'S LADDER

BECOMING THE CHANGE I WANTED TO SEE

chapter

two

A Praying Grandmother

JEREMIAH 29:11 AND JEREMIAH 1:5

For I know the plans I have for you, declares the Lord, Plans to prosper you, and not harm you, plans to give you hope and a future.

Before I formed you in the belly, I knew you. Before you came forth out of the womb, I sanctified you. I have appointed you a prophet to the nations.

I was born on January 19, 1997, in Chicago, Illinois. My grandmother told me a story about my birth, and it was not filled with a warm and fuzzy beginning. You know what's funny? It was only a few months before writing this book that I learned of my birth story. I had suspected it was not a happy day for my parents, possibly because of all of my health problems. I would like to think that they were not unhappy but maybe scared, and that can make sense to me.

When I was born, I didn't just have one condition but several. Being born into this world was a fight and a miracle performed by God. I wasn't healthy at all.

I was diagnosed with mild cerebral palsy, epilepsy, and seizures. What young mother or father could hear this and not be reasonably scared or at the least concerned about how they would take care of me? My mother could have aborted me before I arrived because she had been warned of the possibilities, but she saw the value in my life and kept me alive.

Her choice and excitement waned quickly as the cares of my conditions weighed heavily on her. If this wasn't enough to alarm my mother, when I was born, my brain was bleeding. The doctors said to keep me in the hospital for care and observation, and my mother didn't fight the doctor's orders.

She, I am sure, was overwhelmed and nervous about taking me home. My mom was distant with me and would lash out in verbally abusive words that made me think maybe I was dropped at birth, and that's why I was bleeding. Could she have acted irrationally and hurt me unintentionally and was living with the guilt?

Although my mom struggled to love me, and my father to love either one of us, I had a praying grandmother who did care and loves me. She told me the bible scriptures she would say over my healing each night. She wrote them down and put that paper with me in my crib at the hospital. She didn't give up on me and showed the power of God and his ability to heal with her faith.

I am grateful that, as she heard the reports of my injuries and medical conditions, she didn't stop praying for me. She was warring for me before I could speak up for myself. She reminded me that it is what God says that is final. One thing about God is that his word will not come back to him void. God's word never fails. Hallelujah!

I was in that hospital bed fighting for my life, but God was fighting the biggest battle to keep me alive and bring me out. I remember thinking, why did I have to go through something like this, and mature with ongoing battles to walk and have a normal life.

What I heard back in response was, "Why not you?" God will put you in a situation and/or circumstance, and bring you through so he can get the glory. We may not want to be this example, but if this is what he wants, let God have his way to see the conclusion of the matter.

I was told of all the things I wouldn't be able to do. How I wouldn't walk, talk, read, work, or drive. I prove all the doctors and family members who doubted the goodness of God everyday. I have a degree, and I am the first in my family to do so, despite all my challenges. I left no excuse but leaned on God to be the power I needed with the thorns in my side daily.

When I am invited to baby showers, people tell me they are expecting a baby, or they have had a baby. The first thing I think and pray is,

"Father, may the baby be healthy." That's truly a blessing to have a healthy baby, even more so than the baby's gender. All children are a blessing, no matter their condition, too.

Even though I can't remember the way I felt at birth, because that was over 20 years ago. I do thank God for me being here and my mom choosing to endure however she could to keep me over the years. You don't have to agree with everything your parents have done to you, to love and appreciate them.

I needed to hear this when I was young, that I was a blessing even with my flaws. I used to ask my biological mother and God, "Why was I born"? As a little child, I didn't know who God was or his plan for my life. My parents made me feel like a mistake and not a blessing.

In Isaiah 54:17, it states, "No weapon that is formed against you will prevail; and you will condemn every tongue that rises against you in judgment. This is the heritage of the servants of Yahweh, and their righteousness which is of me," says Yahweh. Whatever circumstance, trial, etc., you may be in, keep pushing through because it will not prosper or cancel your reason for being here.

You may ask yourself, "What if it prospers?" One question you have to ask yourself: Do you believe God's word? God didn't say that it wouldn't form and the words we heard or the emotions we feel wouldn't be very convincing, but he called the notions a liar and smaller than the hand of God. Whose word will you believe?

God knew us before we were formed in our mother's womb (Jeremiah 1:5). When I think about that, I can say that we have to trust the one who formed us. Why worry? Worrying is worshiping satan. Who are you worshiping and where is your faith? Faith is what pleases God, you know?

God knew about us before we were formed in the womb. I can just shout when I think about that. There's a purpose for our lives from God. As my big sister, Dr. K Lee, states in Embrace Your Crown: Open 7 Gates to Find and Overcome Heartbreak, "We are born on purpose, with a purpose, for a purpose". Thank you, Dr. K Lee, for that revelation and God for giving it to you! You are the best!

When I thought about being a newborn and sometimes when I think now, I ask myself, "Why didn't God just take me at birth?" When life is hard and seems to not get better, we can think looking for the exit is better than growing through the pain. He has a purpose for my life and I want to tell you, yours too.

If you question leaving this earth, know you are not alone. Ending your life could seem right, but I want to tell you that is "not" God's plan. He wants me to tell you my story to help you build strength to live your story and become the change you need to see!

Life is a gift. Life is worth living when you have God in your life and something to look forward to. Build a relationship with him as you would with someone you love and care about.

Jacob Bramlett

A relationship with God is the most important relationship to have in this life. God will never leave nor forsake you (Deuteronomy 31:8).

JACOB'S LADDER

BECOMING THE CHANGE I WANTED TO SEE

Jacob Bramlett

chapter

three

The Child Who Was Not in Place

JOHN 15:18

"If the people of this world hate you, just remember that they hated me first."

Growing up, I was oftentimes depressed, but I did have some good days where I was a happy little boy from time to time. I didn't feel happy because I felt the warmth of love; I felt happy because I found things that brought me joy or made me smile. It wasn't until I found the love of God as a teenager that I knew what love was.

All I knew was that I had some favorite cousins —Desanika A.K.A. Coosey, Derek, and Anfernee A.K.A. Twill —who made life fun for me. I can't forget my boy David, who I hung around with a lot as a kid. Keep reading to see how our adult lives turned out.

33

Growing up, all I knew was food stamps, Section 8, no job, asking or robbing Peter to pay Paul. Financial instability was a heavy theme in my upbringing. Living in the projects, with everything you see, you start to normalize the activities around you. I thought it was normal to live like this and that everywhere else was just like this.

"Delaney" Projects in Gary, Indiana–if Gary didn't already tell you a mouthful, was where I called home, or in slang, "my hood"—a place where rent was $100 or less because of Section 8. I don't know if the program really makes people's lives better or gives them an excuse too often. Abuse of a system can always happen, like proper use. I trust the good always outweighs the bad, too.

Have you noticed that poverty seems to have a smell? It smells like musk, and it is thick and sticky. It's not just visible to the eyes or sticky to your touch; it is also in the mind. Poverty is a mindset that is also a learned condition. To overcome poverty, you must allow your reality to blossom with positive and mind-altering experiences that point to more.

Poverty is easily a curse that limits families and generations. Poverty is a thief that steals dreams and strangles hope. God does not want us to settle for less. If we want what God wants for us, we have to open our hearts and minds to experience more.

Some of us want to be homeowners, business owners, write and publish books, or do something that points to a greater existence than where we live. We cannot get there with a low vibrational mindset. You cannot elevate in life if you are still trying to pour new wine into old wineskins. The concepts of freedom in a poverty mindset will only burst the bags holding your dreams. You have to be willing to change how you think and how you live to achieve more.

I didn't understand things as a child. I didn't see that hard work led to progress or a better life. I saw more people working on doing nothing and finding a means to survive. Imagine experiencing abuse and neglect while witnessing poverty.

There is no purse, bag, food, room with a television, or anything to distract you from the pain. It is just yelling and silence. I thought it was the end of the world for me. I considered this was all there was to life, and if it was, why be here? If you thought that life would be better at school than at home, it was another disappointment.

Children are honest, but can also be so mean. They can make jokes and spew comments on things they know little about or may not care about. I went to school with torn-up shoes and dirty clothes all the time. I cannot say why, only that that was the case. As a kid, although school had its problems with people making fun of me, cracking jokes, and thinking I was dumb, it was better than going home.

I never wanted to go home because I knew there was no running water or lights there. I knew I could eat a hot meal at school and that some teachers did check on me as best as they could. I never understood why power and water were such a challenge to maintain.

I hated people seeing my struggle when there was nothing I could do about it. My parents didn't think to do preemptive care, but were reactionary. If I got sick or injured, they would take me to the hospital. But basic maintenance, like visiting the dentist or annual appointments, they would happily miss.

I never went to the dentist, but always went to the doctor because I was having seizures back-to-back as a child. The kids at the school used to always call me "butter teeth" because I was experiencing neglect. The whole time, they didn't even know a toothbrush and toothpaste were a luxury.

There were plenty of times I used to steal a toothbrush and toothpaste at a corner store to take to school with me so I could brush my teeth at school. That was the only way I could brush my teeth. I thank God that I experienced those things as a child because when I have a child in the future, my main priority is to make sure my child is well taken care of physically, emotionally, and spiritually. I did feel bad for having stolen what I had, but I also felt like I had no other choice. The sad part was that stealing and brushing with what I had didn't change anything.

I still remember having seizures as a child. It is not a good feeling. It would start with my body shaking continuously and uncontrollably all over. I would foam at the mouth, and there were times I could swallow my own tongue. My health was not perfect, my living wasn't perfect, and my mother felt she didn't have the perfect solution to care for me. That day, my mother called my grandmother, Ms. Smith, as I was being rushed to Methodist Hospital in Gary, Indiana.

If I knew Jesus, I would have called on the name of Jesus. He's a healer of everything. In John 14:14, Jesus states, "**If you ask anything in my name, I will do it.**" If I knew Jesus at the time, I would have asked the Lord to heal my body from seizures.

But thank God I had a praying Grandmother who could believe for me. I know it was her prayers that covered me. You have to put your faith and trust in Him. If you put your trust in man, even in doctors alone, they will fail you. If you put your trust in the Lord, he will not fail.

Jesus states in Matthew 11:28-30, "**If you are tired from carrying heavy burdens, come to me and I will give you rest. Take the yoke I give you. Put it on your shoulders and learn from me. I am gentle and humble, and you will find rest. This yoke is easy to bear, and this burden is light**."

We have to trust him and believe what he says because his words never fail. Thank God for Jesus rising from the dead after three days. Death could not hold Jesus down. Do you believe Jesus is the Son of God and that He died for your sins? Jesus died and rose up on the third day. Jesus is the only way.

I know I can get carried away talking about my Savior because I know what he has done for me. He covered me when my mind was too young to know that I was in danger. When I was around 8 and 9, my cousins and I had already been exposed to gang activity in our projects. We knew how to gang bang, and we spent a lot of time outside running and playing cops and robbers. It seemed harmless, but it really was programming.

Twill, Justin, and Derek were always around me, even at school. The four of us went to Watson. What I remembered most about the school was that it was an all-boys school. Even the teachers and staff were all male. If I think about it, it could seem a bit like jail, although it was a public school, because of its lack of interaction and diversity.

I remember the nicknames I had in the hood growing up. The adult males, who call themselves "thugs," would call me "Lil G," short for little gangsta. It didn't bother me, and I thought it was a term of endearment.

Later on, I learned handshakes, which likely were codes and signals that I didn't know enough about. I started teaching and promoting the handshakes at school because I was good at it. I picked up the language and would use words like "GDN" and "vicelord". I am not sure of what they mean now, but growing up bore importance to gang life.

I picked up my sense of style from the streets, too. I sagged my pants, walked with my own kind of lean, and my cousins fell into the same way of life. We never questioned what we were taught to do. We just blindly followed, thinking this was the best or only way. School was there, but so much of what we saw all day, every day called it a lie.

If you ask where our fathers were, I could quickly reply, not around. All of our fathers were doing ten plus years in prison. The hood was a lonely place because people didn't stay out long. It was a lot of neglect, and the pressure on the women was hard. To raise boys who were being trained by other males around them, who at some point had a stronger voice than a mother, was hard for her to stop alone.

With no father at home, we turned to the thugs in the street to train us. They told us to chase women, sell drugs to make money, and be loyal. All of which made sense to our young ears. They showed us how to sell drugs, how to hit on women, and even gave us books with sexual content to prepare us for being alone with girls. We were growing up fast and didn't know it.

You have to be careful what you pour into the youth. A child should stay a child for as long as they can because it develops their imagination and ability to dream. Robbing children of this learned experience takes the essence of a child away. It can make them unfocused, limited, and uninspired.

Speak positivity over your children and those you meet. Speak life over their future and dreams. Feed your child nothing but positivity because it will make a difference and help to fight the other things they hear on a regular basis.

Jacob's Message

DO NOT EXPOSE YOUR CHILD TO THINGS THEY ARE NOT SUPPOSED TO SEE. BE CAREFUL WHO YOU LET AROUND YOUR CHILD. YOU DO NOT WANT THEM TO SEE THINGS THEY ARE NOT SUPPOSED TO SEE. IT WILL DAMAGE THEIR BRAINS AND WILL AFFECT THEM MENTALLY AND EVEN SPIRITUALLY.

While in school, I always made the honor roll. I took plenty of tutoring and language arts classes to achieve this. I didn't believe in bad grades. I always thought I could make God happy by doing well in school. I always had my head in the books. The love I had for education as a child was amazing. It was a great escape, even though I saw it as a fantasy in part. I loved education more than chasing girls, but that wasn't the assignment.

I forced myself to chase females to the point that I got in trouble. I always wanted to talk to a girl, but I got dissed for years because of my disability. They used to call me a "special needs" little boy.

One year, I was wearing crutches and braces on my legs. My muscles in my legs started to get weak because of the illness I had. People laughed and talked about me, especially at school.

During that time, I was in special education because of my reading comprehension skills. I was on a 1st grade reading level while I was in the 6th grade. Taking speech classes was well-needed for me every week. I had to take advantage of the speech classes that were held in the school to become a better reader. Any words that start with a "TH" sound were hard for me to pronounce until I was in the 8th grade.

You may ask me, how are you writing a book? You just never know what God can do in your future. I participate in a weekly book club, and I read out loud for everyone to hear. People just don't know how hard I worked to be able to read.

How long I had to fight through the laughter and empty thoughts of if I was good enough. But God knew my story, from beginning to the ending—and he knows yours, too. He will use some circumstances in your life to build and develop you. You are a work in progress, but stay in the process.

People gave me names such as "cripple boy, retard, and "rechargeable legs". Nobody wanted to be my friend because I had a disability. That had me go into a deep depression at the time. The whole time, they didn't know I was dealing with depression outside of school, too.

To be rejected at home and then at school was hard on me. The streets were the only place I felt a resemblance of love, and that wasn't real, either. I was thirsty for genuine love.

I felt hated as a child. During that time, I didn't feel loved by my parents or by anyone. I have never in my life heard the phrase "I love you" from one of my parents. There's a word Jesus stated that I wish I knew as a child.

In John 15:18-27, Jesus states, *"If the people of this world hate you, just remember that they hated me first. If you belonged to the world, its people would love you. But you don't belong to the world. I have chosen you to leave the world behind, and this is why its people hate you. Remember how I told you that servants are not greater than their master. So if people mistreat me, they will mistreat you.*

If they do what I say, they will do what you say. People will do to you exactly what they did to me. They will do it because you belong to me, and they don't know the one who sent me. If I had not come and spoken to them, they would not be guilty of sin. But now they have no excuse for their sin. Everyone who hates me also hates my father. I have done things no one else has ever done. If they had not seen me do these things, they would not be guilty. But they did see me do these things, and they still hate me and my Father, too."

This is why the Scriptures are true when they say, "People hated me for no reason." I will send you the Spirit who comes from the Father and shows what is true. The spirit will help you and will tell you about me. Then you will also tell others about me, because you have been with me from the beginning."

What makes us different from Jesus? We are not perfect. People will hate us, just because. People will talk about you because they have talked about The Lord. Jesus was the ONLY perfect person, and he, too, didn't have a perfect experience here on earth filled with love and acceptance.

So it's okay if you can understand a journey similar to Christ, rather than a false sense of a perfect life. Our struggles are ours, but he comes to heal us of our wounds, hurts, pains, and scars. There is a brighter day; keep reading to see the sunshine.

JACOB'S LADDER

BECOMING THE CHANGE I WANTED TO SEE

chapter

four

When I Found God

PROVERBS 22:6

"Train up a child in the way he should go, and when he is old he will not depart from it."

While I was attending Fairhaven Baptist Church, an "old-fashioned Bible-believing Church" located in Chesterton, Indiana, I was faithful to the Church. I loved learning about God. Nobody in my home told me about him, so I went out and found God on my own. As a child, I used to always see the Fairhaven buses driving around the neighborhood I was living in at the time.

My parent told me to never talk to a stranger. I felt like I was being a disobedient child when I talked to this man, who was a part of the church. I felt God was mad at me for not obeying my parents. The man from the church came to our home and invited me to come. All I remembered from him being there was, "The church bus will be here at 9:45am sharp." I was so excited to go to church.

I was the only individual in my household who attended church. As of today, I am still the only one who attends church to learn more about God and to build my relationship with him. I enjoyed church as a child, even though the church was far away from my home. Thank God for the transportation they had to get people there, or else I would have missed out.

What is church? A church is a gathering of people who will talk about God's word. A church is not a building. You can have church in your own home, restaurant, or even outside. The church is the body of Christ, and the people are the church of God. We are to gather and assemble, but the location is anywhere the Lord is.

I loved hearing preaching. It was something about hearing the word of God that gave me hope to live on. I wasn't as passionate about the other elements of the service, but the preaching made me want to go faithfully every Sunday. It was quickly the only reason I wanted to go, and I came prepared with my Bible on me. I grew to love my Bible so much that I even started carrying it to school to read it there.

Going to church and reading my Bible wasn't a trivial matter to me; it was stronger than magic

—it was the power of God sent to deliver me — to help me. I couldn't stop myself from searching the scriptures. I knew and believed that the power of God was bigger than my circumstances, no matter what they were. Kids still laughed at me, but now they had a new reason, because I was a believer!

At the age of 11, I remember a sermon where the preacher stated, "If you are not saved, you will go to hell. If you are saved, have Jesus Christ, you will live with him forever." I didn't understand what hell was as a child. I know that I loved God. The preacher described two places, "Heaven and Hell," and I knew hell wasn't for me.

It was at the age of 11 that I chose to receive Jesus Christ as my Lord and Savior. I was so happy that I did it. I have faith and still have faith in God. Jesus rose from the dead on the third day, and he's still living on the inside of me and all who believe.

Me and my cousin David, James (Lil J), and I were so close as kids. We used to go to this Bible club every Saturday in the Summer. We were little kids learning about the Lord. I truly appreciate that Bible camp because it led us in the right direction.

At the age of 12, I remember speaking with my uncle Ronald, who was a Jehovah's Witness. There was a line he always stated, "We are living in the last days. We are going to die any minute from now." I started to get worried all of a sudden.

I understood many things because of all of

the things I experienced. The whole time, I should have stayed in the child's place, but I did not have an option. I was forced into aging because of the things I was forced to do that I did not have any business doing as a child. Actually, I was 21 mentally while I was 12.

He invited me to the Kingdom Hall in Gary, Indiana. I was really confused about the faith they had. After attending the Kingdom Hall for a month, I started losing my faith. I didn't want to go there ever again. The spirit in that place couldn't be felt. If I walked in that Kingdom Hall today, I would have told them the truth within the congregation. The truth shall set you free. I just hope that false prophets will learn the error in their ways and do better afterward.

Being a Jehovah's Witness is so complicated to me and the Gospel is simple. I'm glad that I didn't pursue my faith in that denomination. There would be so many challenges within my faith for sure. I know I would have had to ask God more questions and to help me with my unbelief.

Jehovah's Witnesses believe that only 144,000 people will enter Heaven. As a child, I was freaking out and so worried because I knew there were 7 billion people in the world. The Jehovah's Witness belief system meant so many were going to hell, and that number is still growing today.

I truly thank God for the faith I have now. If you are struggling in your faith, ask God to increase your faith in Him. Trust God through your process. One thing for sure: embrace your journey.

During my life journey, I came to the realization that God wants to be involved in my life. He wants to be involved in his kids' lives. There were plenty of times that I was making some life decisions without God's consent. In some situations, I did not know the outcome until the decision was executed.

If you are not sure where you can find God, open His word. You can start in the books of Matthew, Mark, Luke, and John. Those are the gospels. Learn about the Lord and let God speak to you through his word. A follower of Christ comes with conviction.

You know you are born again by the things that you do. Jesus knows you because you are a keeper of his commandments. Do you have his DNA? In this life, you have to humble yourself, just as the Lord, Jesus, humbled himself as our example, too.

How is your relationship with God? Have you read his word? Do you talk to him throughout the day? Or do you only talk to him when you need something?

If so, you need to do some self-evaluation. God did not forget to wake you up this morning. So talk to him. Thank God for the blessings He has given you. Ask God to work some things out in you so you can become the person he meant for you to be.

I want to tell you a quick story about prayer. I am going to jump ahead a bit, but on this occasion, I was praying at 3am. I remember wanting to get a car, but I was uncertain what to ask for. I asked for what was popular in my hood at the time, a 2004 Chevy Monte Carlo Coupe. I loved small cars with 2 doors. I always wanted that car, although I didn't know how or where I would get it from.

It was hard to find that specific car online, even to look at it. There were no other cars I wanted, though, that matched the excitement I had for this car. One year after I asked God for that car, he blessed me with a "BMW" that was a gran coupe.

I was asking God one small thing, and he blessed me with something that was way bigger than what I asked. I share this story to show you that although what you prayed for might take time, it is always worth the wait when you get it. It will be more than you asked, but everything you wanted. God is that *good*!

Learn to trust God in everything. Not just the small things, but the grand things too. Know that his plans are better for you than even the ones you have for yourself. The Bible tells us that his ways are higher than our ways.

We do not serve a little God, we serve a *"BIG"* God. What do you expect God to do in your life? I understand material things do not mean everything in this life. Do not get me wrong, we have to appreciate the things we have. But, ***Do not make MATERIALISTIC THINGS your GOD***, though. Keep your faith in God and keep your eyes on Him.

Above everything else, I thank God that my faith is strong in him. Growing up with a man in the household, my siblings' father, I thought he was God. You may ask, why? My siblings' father told me and all his kids he was God.

All I could ask my younger self, "If he was God, why do he always cut you off when you speak? Why did he lead you to do things that we were not supposed to be doing?" I truly thank God that I found Him on my own. I learned that God is not a person; he is a spirit.

What is wrong with people who think they are God, anyway? I got to tell you, "Don't play with God like that because bad things happen." Choose instead to acknowledge his power and influence on the earth. Choose to see what so many can miss when they are too busy or high-minded to see the writing on the wall.

You have to humble yourself and come to repentance to get enlightened by God. He doesn't put his precious essence in places he doesn't intend to fill to maintain his presence. Faith, humility, love, understanding, self-control, and watching what you say have a place of importance to God.

JACOB'S LADDER

BECOMING THE CHANGE I WANTED TO SEE

chapter

five

When I Felt I Was Job

JAMES 1:2

"My brethren, count it all joy when you fall into various trials."

On September 17, 2016, I felt like I was in the worst nightmare ever. On that day, I was getting ready to go to the job I had at the time. I was working for a grocery store, and it was a good experience and company to work for. It was my first labor job at the time, after teaching early childhood, and I thanked God for an income.

While showering, I saw smoke coming from under the bathroom door. I heard the smoke alarms going off. At the time, my older brother and I were living together; it was our first apartment. So, I rushed out of the shower because I saw the fire on the walls! I was freaking out and screaming loudly. At the time, I didn't want to panic or anything like that, but I thought I was going to die.

Smoke was all over and throughout the apartment. I couldn't breathe at the time, and I knew this was a sign my life was going to end. You may ask, was it really that bad and so quickly? I was inhaling so much smoke that it made me lightheaded. It made me wanna fall through the fire I was surrounded by.

I was coughing so badly, and my eyes were burning at the time. I couldn't see anything. All I could do at the moment was call on God. How many of you can call on God and know God will be right by your side?

At the time, we were on the third floor of our apartment building. Yes, we were high. Before signing the lease, I expressed my concerns about a third-floor unit. I didn't want to have an apartment on the third floor because I was scared of heights. I didn't know what would happen in the future while we were living there. Although I assumed I could struggle looking out on the balcony, I didn't predict a fire that would lead me there.

While I was surrounded by fire, I saw the window cracking from the smoke and heat. Without hesitation, I jumped out of the window. I was scared before I jumped and during the moments I was floating in the air. I was in a lot of pain when I landed, but with the power of God, I got up and shook off the pain. Adrenaline was pumping, and all I could say was, "Thank you, God!"

At the time, after jumping out of the window from the third floor, trying to escape the smoke and fire, I just had underwear on. I was half naked. I didn't have any shoes, pants, or a shirt on at the time. I felt embarrassed. There were people at the apartment complex looking at me crazily.

The aftermath was wild. After the firefighters fought the fire. My brother and I walked through the apartment. Everything was destroyed. At the time, I was full of joy because, as it states in **James 1:2, "Count everything as joy."** While walking through the apartment, I was full of joy because I was walking.

I walked into my room after the fire, and the Bible I had at the time was untouched. There were no burn marks on the Bible. The Bible wasn't ***touched!!!!!!!!!!!!!!!*** The only wish I have is that I still had that Bible. The Bible was lost when I lost everything again at a different point of my life.

My brother wasn't joyful as he walked; he was so mad and angry. We didn't cause the fire, but the child next door to us, who was playing with matches, started it. I wasn't mad about the incident because I knew what I had lost and what I had kept. If anything's lost, I will get it back soon.

I thank God that my brother's mother let us stay with her until they had another apartment for us. I didn't have anything; I just had God to get me through that trial. At the time, we didn't have rental insurance. I didn't know anything about rental insurance during that time of my life. If I had known, I would have had rental insurance at the time to cover what we had lost. Thank God for experiences because experience can be our greatest teacher.

Me and my brother's relationship was somewhat "ok" while living with each other. We didn't really communicate with each other while living under the same roof. We had a dry-erase marker board that we communicated through. I made sure I had stocked up on the dry-erase markers so we could communicate through the board we had in our living room.

Every time I spoke to him face-to-face, he always turned his back on me and ignored me while we lived with each other. At the time, I asked God, Why do I have to live like this? The only way I could get a response from him was through the board that we had. If I needed to tell him something, I had to write it on the board. The response could take hours, days, weeks, etc. Sometimes there was no response at all.

For days, there was no response from him. The two of us living with each other was so frustrating, and stayed stressed out all the time. I only wanted a response to things I needed to know. It was normal for me to talk to a brick wall and not be able to communicate with him. At the beginning of our lease, when we got a second apartment, we made a promise/contract as we did when we got our first apartment.

That promise was that we would split the rent each month, as we did with the other apartment. Our rent was $700 at the time for a two-bedroom. We paid $350 each month; these kinds of rental prices don't exist at all in the times we live in now.

After 3 months of living in the unit, there was an eviction notice on our door. I did not understand why, because I know I paid $350 every month. I had gotten my receipts every time I dropped the money order off at the leasing office.

I remembered asking him, "What is going on? Why do we have an eviction notice?" He did not respond. He asked me questions. When I would answer his questions, he cut me off. That day, he packed all his stuff and left the apartment.

I was in deep thought—some things I did not know what to do. I couldn't pay all the debt because my income wasn't enough. I was left to pay the apartments a little over $5,000 because the lease was broken at the beginning, and the debt that was behind needed to be paid. That debt, which was within that $5,000, included damages to the apartment. There were so many late fees and court costs that the bill was outrageous. I had to figure out how I was going to pay that debt all on my own.

My brother always had alcohol in our apartment because he was a heavy drinker and also smoked. It was days that I drank alcohol so I wouldn't feel how I was feeling. The feelings I felt that I did not want to feel. It was days I drank alcohol to the point that I wanted to be numb. People did not understand me, and I did not really understand what I was dealing with at the moment.

It was days, I used to steal one of his guns out of his room. I always kept one between my mattress for protection. He always had people running in our apartment daily. He never listened to me or wanted to hear what I had to say about this. You have to be very careful who you let into your home. Because you don't know what spirit they are carrying within them that can come into your home.

In my room, I always had the door locked. To the point, I got the gun I had gotten out of my brother's room and set it right next to me in my bed. All I know is my door was kicked in by one of his friends while I was asleep and I determined to be prepared if there was a next time. I felt like I couldn't have any peace in the home where I paid bills. People had abandoned my trust by how they treated me.

I was working endless hours. I know I couldn't get another apartment because of the eviction on my credit. I stayed with my mom and my siblings' dad at the time. I really regretted how I was treated in the past and how I was treated during that time. That was the only option I had at the time. It felt like I was sliding on thin ice within a fire.

As of today, I do not have a very good relationship with my brother. All we can do as disciples of Christ is to pray for people and wish them the best. Do not wish bad on anyone because the bad wishes on the next person can be put upon you. We have to learn to let things go and let people be.

How many of us feel like we lost everything and just need to lean on God? God knew that was going to happen, but we didn't. In that circumstance, I can say that it has taught me a lesson that I have to just lean on him because **"He's the beginning and the end" (Revelation 22:13). We have to trust the Lord, and we can "not lean on our own understanding" (Proverbs 3:5-6)**.

When I was working, I couldn't work so many hours because it was a law I had to follow. I was still receiving a disability check (SSI). I was only receiving $733 a month. I could only working 15 hours a week, 60 hours a month.

I wish I could talk to my younger self and tell my younger self, "Stop depending on the government to provide for you." At the time, I could not have a bank account with a balance over $300 because Social Security could track it and cut off my benefits. During that time, I was also receiving food stamps.

The job I was at held a fundraiser and raised $1,500 for me because of what I lost in the fire. At first, I didn't want to accept it because I believed that I could do everything on my own. I believe in being independent, but I learned interdependence. I was grateful for it and I thanked God for the blessings.

That job was good to me and I will never forget it. I missed teaching but I couldn't do it anymore. I left the teaching field because they weren't paying me enough at the time.

I wasn't paying any federal taxes at the job I was at. I didn't know the importance of that at the time, nor did I know that was the case until 2 years after working there. I never checked my check stubs because I was receiving the same check amount every week.

Two years and some change went by, and I started getting notices in the mail about owing the IRS. I was nervous because the word "federal" was in the letter. I worked it out, but with interest owed, I am still paying the government their money "till" this day. I learned an incredible lesson that could have been avoided.

If I had questions about the check stubs, I couldn't ask anyone because I knew for a fact that I will get ignored, especially at the job I was at. I couldn't ask any relatives, because I would've got cut off when I spoke. My words didn't matter all the years I lived.

If I could turn the hands back on time, I know I couldn't ask people questions or express concerns about things I was going through or dealing with. The fact on how I knew that, was I would always get shut out, cut off, or ignored because I was misunderstood. As of this day, I am still misunderstood, babied, or ignored. When I explain things, nobody understands me, I feel. So I listen more than I speak.

Always getting cut off when I speak, that is the life of a prophet, I hear. A prophet has discernment of things that they see and deal with on a daily basis. It's sad that often they are ignored because people don't want to hear what they have to say.

I never questioned God for the circumstances I was experiencing. All I know is that there was a reason and purpose to things to make me into a better individual. **I was counting everything as joy (James 1:2).** Count everything as joy because all is well. Just say "it's all good", one of my sayings as a child.

I went through a season during 2019-2020, for exactly 11 months, where I was physically homeless. I had no one to lean on. Sleeping outside in the cold, I hated myself. I was homeless during the whole entire winter. Thinking I was helping people financially by covering their bills, car notes, and food expenses while being homeless. That wasn't the case. I was being taken advantage of by individuals who didn't help me when I needed help.

I asked people for help by letting me stay with them for a month or two while I get back on my feet. It was hard for me to get an apartment because of the eviction that was on my credit. The people I have asked are the people I helped financially when they asked for help. Being in that dark place had me questioning God.

I will never wish my worst enemy sleeping outside on the curb, asking for money because I've been there. I felt like life wasn't worth living. Thank God I had some employment at the time, which was only giving part-time hours. How many of us feel like we are at our lowest and want to give up on life? I asked God to help me through what I was dealing with and give me strength.

During those days, I had a Planet Fitness gym membership for $10 to take showers and brush my teeth there. I also had a locker to put my belongings there. During that season of my life, I did not know what to do.

I lost everything again that I had after my sibling's father physically kicked me out of their house. I only had the clothes on my back and a bookbag. I had to leave everything I had behind and live on the streets. One word that my siblings' father told me that I will never forget was, "I hate you, little dude, do not come back to my house."

During that time of my life, I was still faithfully going to Church. I didn't let my situation be known to people because I felt I was a burden to others. I thank God for seeing me through the situation. I always wanted someone I could lean on for some kind of support. God was the only one there at the time.

When I asked for support, the sayings and questions I have been told, I will never forget. These sayings left a pain in my heart. The questions and sayings were, "You are a burden, Jacob. Why are you talking to me? I wish you were dead. Why are you not dead yet? Stop talking to me before something happens to you."

I had to wait 28 years for the support and love I always wanted. As an individual, you have to embrace your journey and keep pressing forward. Never look back.

JACOB'S LADDER

BECOMING THE CHANGE I WANTED TO SEE

Jacob Bramlett

chapter

six

Relationship

JOHN 13:34

"But I am giving you a new command. You must love each other, just as I have loved you."

The things I know now, I wish I knew back then. Have you ever heard that saying before? We all have. If not, you will keep living life longer. We may have told ourselves or someone that "Life is a journey, and we will make mistakes in this journey we are on." Thank God for wisdom and understanding from situations and/or circumstances we face.

At the age of 15, I was living with my dad, his girlfriend Danielle, and her two daughters at the time. This was after I got adopted from being neglected for over a decade. I truly thank God for Danielle. She and her daughters, D'Vaya and Destine, will always have a special place in my heart. I'll always love them because they accepted me and adopted me at the time. I was getting so used to not getting hurt while living with them. I was safe, but Danielle wasn't. Growing up, I was learning that a man was supposed to hit on a woman because I had always seen it as a child.

Thank God that I saw better as I got older, and that taught me differently. It was very different and something to get used to living with mainly women, since my dad was never at the house. I know I was loved by them, and I need that. I learned how a woman is supposed to be treated by living with them. A woman should be treated with respect at all times.

I remember my dad asked me a question when I was under his wing. I was scared and nervous because of what I was used to. He asked me, "Son, why don't you have a girlfriend? Are you gay?" When he asked me that question, I got upset because he asked me if I was gay.

I was explaining to him that no girl likes me because of the way I walk. There is a limp when I walk that I will always have. At the time, I was getting so uncomfortable talking about it because I knew that no woman would want me. The whole time, he didn't know what I was dealing with mentally and emotionally. There was pain inside of me that had built up for years because he had been gone for over 10 years in prison.

It was one night, me, my dad, and my cousin Patches, had taken a drive and talked. The whole time, I was scared because I wasn't so used to venting to men besides God. My dad asked me a question that I answered softly. He told me, "Go find you a woman, or I will find you one. I'll find you some cheeks." That night, my cousin Patches was telling my dad that they should find a woman for me, gave me $40, and told me to go see what woman they had for me.

Back then, I did not understand what was really going on. I did not really understand what the money was for. I declined what they wanted me to try or do with a woman they wanted to see me with. My dad handed me some condoms, but I looked at him *crazy* and told him to take me home. What he gave me, I left in his vehicle. I didn't know what it was used for.

They were mad at me because I did not give in to what they wanted me to do with the $40. That night, they called me a "weak nigga." As of today, I can say they were trying to turn me into a sexual predator. That is so disgusting to really think about. Nothing but sexual perversion that can be avoided. Soul ties are real. You know?

So it was this one light-skinned girl I have liked since 1st grade. I felt like she had my heart. The whole time, I didn't have guidance in getting a woman. I tried my best to the best of my ability with no success.

This girl was my favorite person back then. I always had my eyes on her. The whole time I was dealing with lust, I didn't even know what lust was back then. Seeing this girl back to back ever since first grade had me in love. I loved big girls during my teen and childhood years. I felt the big girls could love me. We met up, and I got her number. I was happy, but the whole time I was nervous because I had never interacted with a female.

When I got home that day, I told my dad. The things he was telling me, I didn't really understand it at the time. He responded, "Good son, now get you a couple more girlfriends. You can bring them over to one of my houses that I have." At the time, I was looking at him crazily. I wasn't too comfortable talking to women at the time. It was nice to have one.

This girl and I started talking. I asked her to be my girlfriend because she made me laugh, and I felt accepted. Weeks later, I started going over to her house to hang out with her. I was feeling so uncomfortable at the time. I wasn't used to being in a woman's present. We played video games with her brothers and even went bowling that night with her family. What a day we all had.

After the day of hanging out with her, my dad asked me a question. This question was so scary to answer because I had never been asked the question before. He asked me, "Did you have sex?' I responded, "No." He asked, "Why not?" I replied, "I believe in waiting til marriage for that."

He didn't believe in marriage, so he was pressuring me to have sex. At the time, I was only 15. I was scared; I didn't know what to do or who I could turn to for better advice.

My father pressured me so badly to have

intercourse with the girl. He stated, "Wear a condom too." He gave me a condom at the time, so I put it in my room. I let it sit on my dresser for so long to the point that I forgot I put it there. I was going to throw it in the trash, but I didn't want to be disobedient to my father.

I didn't throw it away that day, but when I did throw it away. My dad asked me, "Who is the girl you lost your virginity to, because I do not see the condom in your dresser?" I did not believe in lying. I always believe that it is always good to tell the truth, although I was raised to lie about everything by a relative of mine, I couldn't do it. I told him that I threw the condom in the trash.

He was so mad at me at the time. It was at that point that he gave me a box of condoms. I did not know how to use it or what it was used for. During that moment, I was so uncomfortable talking about those things.

My dad told me, "Find a girl so I can drop you off to her." So I hit up the girl that I had my eyes on for so many years. The conviction in my spirit that I had at the time I was feeling so uncomfortable to the point I couldn't breathe.

About the time I was 17, I was so mad at myself because of the decision I had made. I had lost my virginity to the girl I had had my eyes on. I told my dad about it, and he was so excited. My step-mother, Danielle, knew about it; she wasn't too happy about it because of the facial expression she gave me. The whole time, I was disgusted and angry with myself because I had broken the covenant. I wanted to wait until marriage, as God wanted us to do. I wish I hadn't listened to my dad, but I didn't want to be a disobedient child.

The girl and I had a good relationship going on. I felt so comfortable around her. For some odd reason, I felt comfortable around her. Years later, it started to get serious. I brought her a promise ring from Pandora. I was so happy. I felt like a happy young man. I told my dad about it. He asked, "You are about to marry her?"

It was that night that I got on one knee and proposed to her with the promise ring. Thinking she was going to be mine forever was in my head all the time. Years later, in August 2019, I brought her an engagement ring that was $800. I was so happy. I had saved up for a long time.

Fast-forward to October. I asked her if she would be my wife, and she said, "Yes." I felt like a lucky man at the time. I had my eyes on her for so many years and wanted her all to myself. I wanted her to be mine because I gave my body to her. Things started to get very serious.

At the end of 2019, I was working two jobs at the time, at a global warehouse and a grocery store. I felt like I was the man. The man who was going to provide for his fiancée. Life was good during that era. The amount of joy I had was unbelievable because I felt like someone accepted me for who I was after being dissed by so many women. I wish someone would have knocked me on the side of the head. I had to learn from this lesson. Thank God for the lesson, too.

There came a day when I didn't hear from my so-called "fiancée." I was getting concerned about her too. She wasn't replying to my texts or phone calls. So when she hit me up a few days later, she stated, "I have a boyfriend, Jacob." I pretended that I didn't hear what she said.

I thought she told me a lie. I told her, "I'm your boyfriend, fiancée, best friend, etc. I'm all in one," I kidded with her. She stated, "No, not you, I'm currently talking to one of your cousins now." I sat on the phone in silence and hung up.

I didn't know how to feel at the time. I was so heartbroken. She had me thinking I wasn't enough for anyone. I was a little dude who was so heartbroken that it led me into a deep depression. I questioned God, was I enough for anyone? Nobody wanted to be my friend. I was questioning my worth daily.

I was planning the engagement ahead of time. I was giving money to her so she could build her savings. I gave her $150 every 2 weeks. Exactly $300 every month. I am thinking about what a fiancé should do for his woman.

I was becoming the change I wanted to see by how I treat people and by doing right by others. It was a time I asked her how much money I had given her that she had saved so far. Her response was, "I am broke, I spent it on someone else's books in jail." I walked out of her home and called for a ride without any explanation.

The moral of the story is that I shouldn't have rushed the engagement. I should not have broken the covenant by having sex outside of marriage. You have to be careful who you lie with. The elders I used to be around as a kid forced me and my cousins to have intercourse with women. I didn't want to be like my dad with six baby mamas. I dislike that term. I would rather say "children's mothers" instead of "baby mamas". I am older than two of my dad's baby mamas.

My dad thinks I would turn out like him as an adult. That's a no-no. I see the bigger picture of things. I want to do right by God. The whole time, I was discerning things. I didn't know what discernment was until I got it in my mid-20s. You may ask, What is discernment? Discernment is the perception in the absence of judgment to obtain spiritual guidance and understanding.

During this period of my life in the middle of 2025, I'm single but desire marriage. There has been only one relationship that I have been in my life til this point. In the generation I am living in now, there are so many red flags.

Red flags, Jacob? Yes, red flags. I'm not rushing to be in a relationship. I'm still waiting for God to send me a wife. I believe I was born in the wrong generation sometimes.

On February 11, 2024, Bishop Steven L. Thompson preached on something I wish I had known sooner in my life. He had a sermon called, "I'm Living Single, But I Desire Marriage." He talked about 20 tips on selecting and accepting a candidate as a mate. The tips he was stating had me in deep thought. It made me want better for myself.

Some of the tips that Bishop Steven L. Thompson stated that had me in deep thought were:

- **You have to know if education matters or not to them.**

- **How does the person of interest care for themselves and currently earn their "viable" living?**

- **Do not think that if you marry someone, you have the power to change them. Changing a person takes repentance, and that is a gift of the Spirit, so thinking you can change them means you have that gift. We don't, only He does.**

- **Lastly, look at why, how, and where the person of interest spends money (Matthew 6:21).**

During the sermon, I was telling God, I hear you, God. I wish I had known these things sooner. During this year of 2025, I have been single for 6 years, going on 7. Technically, it feels like I have been single my whole life.

While being single, God exposed so much to me about relationships. There are plenty of toxic relationships. People are cheating on each other. So many diseases are going around. Why don't people believe in staying committed to one individual? I do not know.

Sex was only for people who are "married."

God did not create sex to be an audition for dating, but a privilege only for marriage. I don't understand why I was forced to do that activity by my dad before adulthood. Why was I exposed to that by my own parent?

I forgave him for leading me in that direction. As of today, he asks me, "Why don't I have kids?" He thinks I'm gay because I don't do what he does. I believe in doing right by God. I thank God that I haven't become what I was taught. The biggest mistake can cost you everything.

For days, I've been thinking to myself, *why would God send me the woman he has for me*? Being in a relationship isn't my big priority right now. Just going to focus on God, building myself, and furthering my education. I believe Education is important. Dr. K Lee stated, "The only thing worse than no education is poor education," in one of her books called "Over The Fact."

Over the Fact

AuthorKLee.com

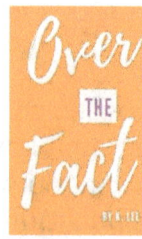 

Marriage is the goal for me in my future. The standards I have when it comes to dating and choosing a woman are that she has to be well-educated. I have to know the woman for at least 10 to 15 years in order for me to marry her.

I think that is enough time for me to know who she really is. Oh and yes, you read it right, 10 to 15 years. I have to be cautious in this world. Ya know?

The one I look to as my mother, Danielle, the one who took me in at the age of 15. I truly thank God for her. She made a big impact on my life. God sent her through my dad to help me in areas of my life. I thought she and my dad were going to be together long term.

If she had never came into my life at the age of 15, I wouldn't be the person I am today; it was because of our talks that I grew, and we still speak from time to time. In May of 2024, I gave her a star of fame for being the best mother. I was thinking about all the things she did for me while I was under her wing. How can I give back?

It's strange that I speak to her about things that I cannot speak to my biological parents about. I speak to her more than I do my biological mother. I always wanted a good, solid relationship with my parents, but it's strange that some parents do not want to have a relationship with their child. Some parents are jealous of their own children. I feel that my parents hate the fact that I beat some odds that they thought I would never overcome because of the illness I was dealing with as a child.

My stepmother, Danielle, was always serious about school. When me and the girls got home from school, we knew that we had to do our homework before we did anything. She really didn't have to worry about my schooling because I was always on top of my studies.

I cannot thank God enough for sending Danielle through my dad. God knows I needed her in some areas of my life. She did an amazing job as a parent. I thank God that I have a relationship with her.

Being an adult, sometimes we get busy with work, home, and life. I appreciate the talks that we have every couple of months. I give her flowers while she is alive. She is one of the greatest mothers that I know. She taught me right while I was under her wings. If I could choose my mother in this lifetime, I would choose her for sure.

On April 5, 2015, at the age of 18, a date I will never forget. On that date, right on Resurrection Sunday of 2015, I rededicated my life to God at Peace Baptist Church in Gary, Indiana. I got baptized!

The most familiar face in the audience was Danielle, right there to witness that I had gotten baptized. I felt like there was so much baggage from my past about what my parents did toward me. I just wanted to let it all go and let God handle what needs to be handled.

Only God knows what Danielle did while I was under her wings. She did an amazing job with me and her two girls. I know it wasn't easy. Dealing with the losses she has experienced with her dad and her uncle had me broken emotionally, spiritually, and even physically. Deacon Ware (her dad) was a great man.

I never felt that way, ever going to other funerals or experiencing loss. During that era, I just wanted to go to my room, lock the door, and didn't want to come out. Losing a parent is a pain that will never go away. This may be strange to some people: I grieve for people that's not even dead. People I want to love now and not just after they are gone.

There are days when some people like me want to call their parents and tell them about their successes or what they have going on in life. After so many years, you have to realize there are a lot of people who are not happy for you. They will pray for you to fail. It's wild when the people you have come from are praying for your downfall.

I have witnessed it behind these eyelids of mine. My own biological parent told me that they hope I fail and that I never existed. It is so painful to hear that from your parents. Do I forgive my parents? Most definitely, I do. I do not believe in holding grudges.

While I was living with my dad and Danielle, he was barely ever home. He was always out cheating with other women who were around my age at the time. Danielle was the main one who made sure I was taken care of. My dad did not have faith in me. I always asked him can he teach me how to drive?

The response was always, "No, you have to learn this one specific thing first in order to drive." When I try to learn that thing as of today, I still don't have the ability to adapt to it. I believe that certain things are not within my calling by God.

Before getting my driver's license, I had my driver's permit for 3 years. Nobody wanted to teach me how to drive. It was always a response of "No." I saved $2000 for a down payment on a car. I just had to go and pick it up.

I asked plenty of people if they could pick up the car for me since I did not have my license. People gave me responses of, "No, go figure it out on your own" or "You will not get that car." I had to ask a deacon at the Church to pick up the car for me.

I am grateful for the deacon who went and picked up the car for me. It was a nice KIA Optima. I was so proud of myself. My car note was only $300 a month.

When the car was driven off the lot, I got in to drive it for the first time. Can you believe that the car I just bought, I never test drove it? I got behind the wheel and was so nervous.

I was telling God, "Forgive me because I am about to drive. I do not know how to drive, but be behind the wheel with me. I know I am driving dirty because I do not have my license. I have to use what you have given me to get where I want to be."

All I know is that when I got behind the wheel, I was driving with two feet. I got on the highway and started doing 80 in a 55. I was so terrified and afraid. I know I have to believe in myself and learn how to drive because nobody would teach me. At the moment, I know I have to teach myself by choosing a different route.

It was August 24, 2021, that I will never forget. It was the day that I got my driver's license. I had left work early and went right up to the licensed branch. One of my coworkers, "Tomeka," went with me to get my license. I knew I needed someone to go with me who had a license. All I remember her saying was, "You better pass."

I passed the driving test on the first try after teaching myself how to drive without any help. There were times I asked people if they could go with me to get my driver's license; the response was always a "No." People did not understand that I needed a licensed driver to get my license. I thank God that it was an individual who said "yes" to help me get what I wanted, my driver's license.

On May 19, 2021, I got my first car, and I was so proud of myself. At the time, we were still in the pandemic, wearing masks and all. The interest rate was outrageous on just about everything. Since I did not have any type of credit, that also didn't help.

Technically, I did have credit, but there were some things on my credit report late payments I did not owe because of Identity theft by a parent. The bank hit me with 29.99% on the car. At the time, I thought that was a good rate on the car. I didn't really understand interest rates at the time.

When others saw me having my first car, there were a lot of individuals asking me questions: "How did you get that car? Are you selling drugs?" Those questions I really disliked. Why do they think that selling drugs is the only way to have something? People's mindsets need to change if they want better.

I thought I had gotten myself a nice car. I didn't know anything about cars. The dealership sold me a lemon. I didn't know what to do after I spent over $1,000 in a period of time getting it fixed. I had to have the spark plugs and ignition coils changed out every week. At times, I had to get the oil change done on that car every week. I felt the car was a "gold digger". So that's what I named her.

As of today, I know things about cars based on my experiences in life. It is crazy that I have to learn things from experiences instead of knowing things from individuals who have already had the experiences. I believe I was created from a different cloth.

There's a time someone was not there when I needed help. I was so alone, like I was all my life. It was time I drove to Gary from Indianapolis to go see my grandmother. I left Gary at 8 p.m. on a Sunday night. I always say a prayer for safety when I drive because you never know what's on the road.

On that Sunday night, while driving, my car was slowing down. The engine light was blinking. After I pulled over, I put the car in park. I got my phone, scrolled through my contacts to see who I could call to help me out because I was stranded. I called about 10 individuals. I called plenty of people.

When I called those people to help me out, the responses were, "I can't help you." "Go figure it out on your own. "Why are you calling me?" "Why are you not dead?", etc.

I will never forget those questions and responses from those individuals because they left a pain in my heart that will never be healed. Before asking for help, I offered them $200 to help me. They did not want to take the offer.

So I had to figure out something. I was in the middle of the road where there were no street lights, just cornfields on I-465 North. I started my car and started accelerating. The crazy part about it is, when I started accelerating, the car could only go 10 miles per hour. I was so frustrated that nobody could be there for me.

I asked God to help me get home safely. I told God I did not understand why nobody would be there for me. The whole entire time, I was there for people financially and emotionally. I was so mad at myself that I did not have anybody.

That night, I told God, "I feel I am all alone, I don't have nobody." I couldn't call my parents at the time because the hate they had towards me was a different story. I did not have a relationship with them at the time.

After making it home the following morning, I was tired. It had taken me 7 hours to drive to Indianapolis from Gary. Technically, the drive is 2 hours if the vehicle did not give me any issues.

While driving home, I got pulled over by the police so many times throughout the night and morning. The officer once asked me, "Do you have roadside assistance with your insurance? Do you have anyone to come help you?"

I told the officer, "I do not have anyone, I just have me. I'm my own team that came into this world alone. But here's my license, registration, and insurance." At that time, I didn't understand auto insurance.

I was paying $180 a month through my provider. My deductible was $2,000. Which is ridiculous. I did not have roadside assistance either. After all of that, the officer said, "I will not give you a ticket or anything. Keep your hazard lights on, and get home safe."

There are two individuals whom I thank God for. There are two women who God blessed me in my life during a season in my life when I was lost, unmotivated, had self-hatred against myself, etc. These women are Ms. Willie and Ms. Maria. God placed them in my life on the job to help me in some areas of my life. They always made sure I was on my P's and Q's. They have children who are older than me.

God only knows they are two individuals I miss dearly. I'm literally shedding tears while I type this. My cousins, Twill and Derek. They were like brothers to me. The relationship we had, I felt safe with them. We were so close. It was like a brotherly love thing.

Sadly, their life was cut short over one small mistake. The biggest mistake can cost you everything. It hurts me to this day to think that if they don't know Christ, where they are now.

If I could turn back the hands of time, I would make sure I tell them about God. The mental state I was in during that time, I wasn't where I needed to be mentally or spiritually. The faith I had at the time was great. The relationship I was building with God was a work in progress to become better. Trying to figure life out was my main priority at the time.

On November 1, 2015, I was sleeping in my dorm room at Philander Smith College in Little Rock, Arkansas. I got a phone call at 1:30 a.m., stating, "Your brother died." I asked, "Which one? What is going on?"

When I heard the response "Twill," I hung up the phone and started screaming and shedding tears. That situation of how he was taken out of this world still hurts me to this day. I still cannot believe he was taken out of this world at the age of 18 on October 31, 2015.

October 31, 2015, is a day that I wish had never existed. On that night my cousin and friend, was killed. On that night, I saw a post on social media that I will never forget. The post text read,

"There was a vehicle that ran into the garage, and the garage collapsed while the car was in the garage. A man came outside and started shooting the victim over 10 times." That post was about what happened to my cousin. He was stealing a vehicle and died trying to do it.

The last time I saw him in person was August 17, 2015, when he and my dad dropped me off to college in Arkansas. Before the road trip to Philander, Danielle told me not to forget my Bible before we left the house. That was the only thing I knew that would protect us from things that we could not see.

The last time I talked to Twill was on October 31, 2015, at 11:35 p.m. That was the time that I hung up the phone. It is crazy that I still have the screenshot of the last phone calls and text messages that we had. I believed he got into that vehicle right after we got off the phone that night.

The last conversation we had is a conversation that I will never forget. We were on the phone, he was telling me how proud he was of me. We were on the phone for 4 hours (from 7 p.m. to 11:35 p.m.). The last words I told him were "I love you, cuzzo, I'll talk to you in the morning."

He responded, "I love you too, cuzzo, I'll be looking forward to you calling me." He knew I loved him. That was truly my ride or die. Sadly, I couldn't attend his funeral because no one ever told me the date of his funeral after I asked.

November 9, 2021, was a day that I felt like I couldn't move on with life. I lost my cousin/brother Derek at the age of 24. Me and this man were always laughing on the phone. I really loved that man. Whenever we talked, we always talked about fatherhood. He was a great father to his first and only daughter.

Derek was the main one who always kept me going. Even though we were 1,000 miles away, the bond we had was something that could not be broken. There were times we would call each other 2 or 3 in the morning to talk about anything. If there was anything I had going on, he always asked and stated, "What I got to do to support you? Let me know."

When I got the call and was told he had passed, my response was, "Stop lying to me, I just talked to him an hour ago. I was literally just on the phone with him on November 9, 2021, at 3:25 p.m. I screamed so loud while I was driving at the time. I wanted to break down while I was driving on the highway. I started speeding on the highway because of how emotional I was.

I made arrangements at my job to take a leave for 3 weeks because of the loss. At the time, I had to decide whether to make the 15-hour drive to see him one last time or not go at all. At his funeral, all I could do was break down.

These two individuals were a big part of my life. We grew up as kids, slept in the same bed together, fought for one another, and even went to the same school with each other. I still remember the days when we attended the David O. Duncan School out in Gary, Indiana, from 2002 to 2005.

As people, we have to be very careful how we treat people. You never know the last time you will see each other. I know one individual once said, "I wish I could tell him something different. I told them, "I hate them."

That individual can develop self-hatred because of how they treated someone they loved, that they cannot reverse. Every time, when me and my loved ones end the day and go to our homes. I always tell them, "I loved them."

There is one individual I will never forget: my little cousin, Desanika, A.K.A. "Coosey." Me, her, and Twill were very close as kids. We all went to school together. We fought for each other in school. I remember one day when we attended "Roosevelt High School" in Gary, Indiana. It was a day that I got jumped by a lot of dudes because I was talking to a girl. The girl I was talking to, I did not know she had two boyfriends at the time.

That day, I saw Twill coming around the hallway, running to the crowd to help me. All I know is he started swinging on those dudes and Coosey as well when she found out what was going on. I felt bad that they had been expelled from school because they were fighting for me that day.

As of today, I wish I could hug Twill, but he is no longer here on earth. I am so proud of Coosey as of today. She is married, with 3 kids, a homeowner, and she graduated from college. God can most definitely work on others if they want to live right. No matter how the past looks, you can never look back. The windshield is bigger on a vehicle for a reason.

Life is too short not to feel loved. I am a living witness to that. I always wanted to be loved as a child. As a child, I begged to be loved and to be appreciated. Tell your people that you love them. God is love. Jesus states in John 13:34, **"But I am giving you a new command. You must love each other, just as I have loved you."** There is no fear in love.

JACOB'S LADDER

BECOMING THE CHANGE I WANTED TO SEE

chapter

seven

Battling With The Enemy

2 TIMOTHY 1:7

"... for God gave us a spirit not of fear but of power and love and self-control."

As a child and preteen, I was always suicidal to the point that I harmed myself because my pain was so deep. I didn't know I was battling with the enemy. I did not know the decision had a penalty. There were plenty of attempts that I wanted to commit suicide. The marks and scars on my body, I still have til this day. I remembered the reasons why I cut myself.

I didn't know where that spirit came from. The whole time, I didn't know it was a spirit I was dealing with. I thought it was normal to deal with the thoughts I had. I didn't care about life at all. Most days, I slept in the room. I didn't want to talk to anyone.

Some nights, I told God to take me away. If he didn't, I would take myself away. Imagine hearing voices saying, kill yourself, you are not going to die, you are not enough, etc., constantly. It was hard dealing with those thoughts. Folks thought I was crazy and weird. As a child, I did not know who I could talk to concerning that matter. All I knew was that I was going to get cut off as I spoke.

It was days, I went to school depressed. My grades started slipping. I didn't even care about anything for some years. I didn't tell my parents what I was dealing with at the time, because I wasn't comfortable talking to them as a child. I didn't even wanna talk with my sibling's father because I was scared of him until I was 14. Me and that man always fought when I was a child, every time he put his hands on me.

Being 10 years old, I was double my age mentally because of the neglect and abuse I was experiencing. The number of things I have seen behind these eyelids of mine has made life move so fast for me. I had to force myself into adulthood. I did not have a choice at the time.

It was during the time I had seizures back-to-back that I wanted to end it all. I remembered having a seizure in front of my sibling's father; he didn't check to see if I was ok or anything. Foam was coming out of my mouth while my body was shaking repeatedly. I was really scared. He laughed at me while I was having a seizure. I felt like life wasn't worth living. Have you felt like the devil was next to you or on your neck? If you have, I can relate because I, too, felt that way. That feeling is horrible and scary, and I don't wish it on anyone.

It was many nights, I slept with a knife in my pocket because I was going to end my life. I don't want to talk about the nights I used to harm and cut myself as a child. The depression I was in was so deep to the point I couldn't feel anything. I remember asking myself as a child, "Is life worth living?" I remember looking things up on the internet, "How to leave Earth on your own? How can I kill myself?" I even told my mother," Take me out of this world," and I asked her, "Why did she have me?"

The crazy part about this is that I still have the marks on my body that I still have from when I was cutting myself. I still remember the reason why I cut myself on each of my body parts that I have cuts on. Some cuts on my body have healed, but many have left scars.

People thought I had been abused physically, but I was the one doing it with knives that I always slept with. There was always blood on the comforters and sheets I was sleeping on. I used to always hide the comforters and sheets because I knew nobody would listen to me as a child.

At the age of 7 til the age of 17, I have always thought someone was behind me. I kept doing a 360-degree turn around everywhere I went. I felt like someone was on my back physically. It literally felt like someone was on my back. I didn't know God before the age of 11.

I didn't know what to do about the moment. I didn't know who I could talk to. I couldn't talk to anybody because I was misunderstood. As a child, my words did not matter. I was always told to shut up as a child.

The way I felt spiritually when I felt the devil was on my back was relentless. I wanted to tell my stepmother Danielle when I was under her roof. I always had the mindset of "**I AM A BURDEN; NOBODY DOESN'T WANT TO HEAR WHAT I HAVE TO SAY. I WILL GET CUT OFF ANYWAY BECAUSE THAT'S WHAT I AM USED TO. MY WORDS DIDN'T MATTER. SO WHY SHOULD I SPEAK?"**

No need for me to tell my dad about the situation. Everything was about "street life" and "looking towards sexual things" when I talked to him about anything. The things I wanted to talk about to him will be so irrelevant to him. I would feel like I was talking to a brick wall sometimes. The response I will hear repeatedly from him is "Get you some booty."

Those thought patterns led me til I was 23 years old. I was dealing with the enemy. Some nights I had to call on the name of "Jesus." One of the most powerful names I had to come to know. Nobody knew what I was dealing with mentally and on the inside but God.

There was so much negative talk that was built up within me over the years. I remembered going to the altar at "God's Grace Community Church" for prayer. I asked one of the deacons to pray over me regarding this situation, as I was dealing with suicidal thoughts constantly. Thank God that I had escaped from that mentality I was brought up in at the age of 23.

I thank God that I am free from that stronghold. Life is worth living if you are thinking about ending your life. Ask yourself this question: What would Jesus do? If Jesus had the power to raise from the dead, heal the blind, heal any sickness, etc. Jesus can heal you mentally, spiritually, and physically.

There is an artist that I listen to named "Rare of Breed." He has a song called "The Devil Is A Liar." That's a big fact. I would rather put my country-style boots on and stomp the enemy right on his neck than shrink to the dark place I was in before.

I was in a season where I was battling with the enemy. The whole time, I didn't even know it. As a child, I always wanted to be dead. I always slept with a knife so I could think about when I would take my life away.

There were nights I cried because I was so deep into depression. I hated myself. During those times, I was living with my mother. I was always isolated from my siblings and everyone. I was always alone.

Some days, I start breaking things that I was given. Back then, I used to destroy the whole house because I was so angry on the inside. I didn't feel loved and felt like I wasn't good enough. While I was a child, my mother would often tell me that she wished she had never had me. I did not understand why she would tell me that. That was the reason why I was planning to take myself out of the world.

When I look back on that situation, people hate the fact that I have beaten the odds. Some never knew that I would be the person I am today. When there are minors who are dealing with suicidal thoughts, hating themselves, depression, etc, I can easily talk to them about how to overcome it. I've been there and know how it feels because I've been in those circumstances. There's a way to overcome those things through prayer. The enemy will do anything to have you hate yourself.

Anxiety is an identity, and fear is an expression. While being suicidal, I used to always think about when I would cut my time away from earth. The fear I had within me, some of the attempts were successful, but not fully successful. I was scared; I always thought God would be mad at me when I was attempting to take my own life.

You may ask, what made you get to that point? Dealing with depression for so long, being hated, not feeling loved, being misunderstood, and always not being heard as a child got me to that point. I knew I had to rush my age when I was forced into doing things that I wasn't supposed to be doing by a parent. What happens when a child is supposed to stay in a child's place? Well, I didn't have a choice. I was forced into adulthood before I got into my teens.

chapter seven: Battling With The Enemy

Back then, over 20 years ago, my sibling's father, with whom I was under the roof for over 10 years, exposed me to some things that my mind couldn't comprehend as a child. He used to always show me a big stack of money every day. I thought that was a great thing. He exposed me and my little brother to a certain thing that was weighed on a scale. I remember a day he taught me how to weigh it and put it in sandwich bags. As of today, I can say that it was "marijuana" or "weed." He used to have so many drugs in the kitchen.

That man should never step foot in my presence, and I mean that. First, he taught me habits that I needed to unlearn. Second, he set his son up to be a thug at a young age. Currently, my brother and his dad are doing time in prison for committing a father-son crime.

You have to look at what you're feeding the youth. If you show them the way of destruction, they will repeat it. **You train a child, the way it should go, and they will never depart from it (Proverbs 22:6)**. If I had obeyed my brother's dad and did what he told me to do, I would be in prison right now, facing 20 plus years with him and his son.

I hate the fact that my little brother's dad led him in the wrong direction. I remember a night I was hanging out with them. At the time, I didn't have any friends. I was just fitting in. I was 20 years old at the time.

I thought these guys were having a great time. I was laughing and joking with them. Then out of nowhere, the mood changed. People started fighting and shooting. As soon as I heard gunshots, I ran home barefoot.

That same night, I was told by my brother's dad not to go to his house and that I had to stay outside. He forced me to hold the glock and attempt to shoot it. The gun was loaded. I failed to shoot it, dropped the gun, and ran in a different direction. While I was running, I heard five gunshots.

My little brother came where I was that night. He was with his child's mother at the time. By the way, my brother was 14 at the time, and his girlfriend was not too much older. He came up to me and asked me if he needed some money for some weed.

During that moment, I didn't know what to say. The whole entire time, he had two stacks of cash in his pocket. I remembered that moment I stated that "He was just like his daddy." Then he said back to me, "Forget you and everything you stand for on GVCL." Whatever that acronym means is related to gangs.

I was on the porch just chilling, watching him and his woman chase each other around. The whole time, I was jealous because I always wanted someone that I could call mine. He and his woman were smoking after my brother got the blunts from his dad. At first, I thought he was going to be up to no good.

I can say I thought wrong at the time. I remember my sibling's dad told me, "Don't tell my kids what to do or give them any advice on how to do things right. I tell them because they are my kids. If you tell them how to do anything right, watch what will happen to you."

During that night, my brother was high on weed (loud) and KD (synthetic weed), he was smoking. He came up to me and was up to something at the moment. He pulled two guns out and pointed one of them at me. I didn't understand the reason he did that. He attempted to rob me in front of his woman and his dad. I had to give up $100 at the time.

I was scared, and I thought I could trust him. There wasn't anyone I could tell about the situation at the time because his dad knew what he was doing, and our mother couldn't say anything to him because of his dad. What his dad said was always final. He was always going to respect his father. Our mother couldn't tell him anything because he was told that he only listened to his dad.

During that moment, while the gun was to my head, I thought to myself, I could have taken that move myself before I let someone else do it. As of today, I forgive my brother for what he has done to me. I felt I was going to die that night. It took me some years to heal from that trauma.

As of today, my relationship with my brother is very shaky. I pray for him. I asked God to change his heart and heal his mind. I don't hold anything against him because we have to learn how to forgive others. You have to forgive people for you. Sometimes it may not be easy, but it will be worth it in the end.

Forgiveness is a business term. You have to forgive people and let it go. It will hurt you in the long run if you do not forgive. I always said this saying "it's all good" when someone did me wrong, betrayed me, stole from me, robbed me, jumped me, etc. Everything is all good because I forgave people and did what I did by doing right by people. Whenever I speak up on things, the response I always get told, "You do not know what you are talking about, Jacob."

In **John 15:20**, Jesus states, **"Remember the word that I said unto you, the servant is not greater than his Lord. If they have persecuted me, they will also persecute you; if they have kept my saying, they will keep yours also**."

Forgive others not because they deserve it, but because you deserve peace. Unforgiveness will make you sick physically. You may ask yourself, "How can I walk in true forgiveness?" You have to acknowledge the hurt, understand the perspective, and release resentment. In this lifetime, people will not forgive you, but you have to live through it. Learn to forgive others!

I never knew this saying until now: God will have you minister to people who broke you, shut you out, and betrayed you. As I stated in my first chapter, "Redemption," no matter what people do to me, I still help them with what they need. I do not believe in holding grudges. You have to forgive daily.

My young brother, who is incarcerated, stole from me, fought me for going against his dad, attempted to shoot me, etc. I still give him advice when he calls me from prison. It doesn't matter what the past looks like. The past is dead and gone. I talked to him as if those situations had never happened. That is true forgiveness.

His dad does not want me to communicate with him because he hates the man that I have become. When we talked, I gave him advice on doing better once he gets released from the system in the future. I still put money on his books from time to time. Do I regret it? No, sometimes you have to do what you have to do.

It was a day in May of 2024 that I had gone to my lil brother's court date. He was involved in a son and father crime. It doesn't make any sense that a parent will lead their child (seed) into destruction. On his court day, when he accepted the plea deal, I had testified on his behalf.

During that moment, I was nervous because I was sitting right next to the judge. Even though I didn't tell the judge anything bad about my little brother, I forgave him for what he had done against me. The judge told me to answer some questions he asked me.

I reversed some questions and statements to the judge. The things I stated were, "You trained a child the way it should go." That's biblical, and that's a big fact. Why would a parent lead and force their child into doing things that are not right? That is not what this defendant is.

His father messed up his life by peer-pressuring him into things that are not good. The questions you have should be towards his father. The company you keep, you will develop into that. The environment you are around, you will be the next statistic of the environment.

After speaking on his behalf, 30 years was cut off his sentencing. Later on that day, he called me from prison and was like, "Thank you, bro, for saving me. I thought I would be away from home for life."

Learn to forgive others today. You wonder why you are always sick physically. It must be because you may have some unforgiveness in your heart. I challenge you to forgive the person that you hate and that has done you wrong. Start to love them.

JACOB'S LADDER

BECOMING THE CHANGE I WANTED TO SEE

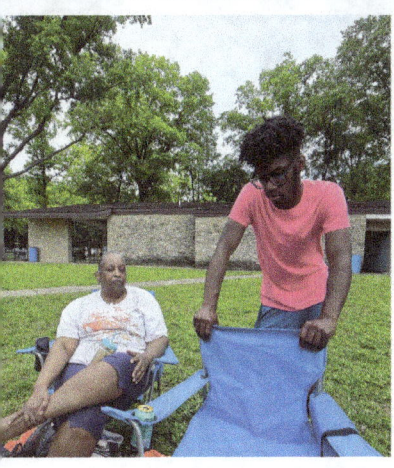

chapter

eight

Material Things are Not Everything, but a Legacy is

1 JOHN 3:17

"But whoever has this world's goods, and sees his brother in need, and shuts up his heart from him, how does the love of God abide in him?"

Comparison is a thief of joy. I cannot get caught up in that. You want to know what is very interesting that will have you in deep thought? Comparison is so dangerous because *you can end up comparing where God has you to where the devil has somebody else*. As my little niece "Zoe" always says, "clock it."

Going through a season where I was comparing myself, I hated myself, and I didn't like what God made me to be. As a child, I compared myself to others. **Proverbs 29:25** states, "**The fear of man will prove to be a snare, but whoever trusts in the Lord shall be safe.**"

At the age of 21, I was comparing myself to other individuals. For instance, I was comparing myself to a cousin of mine. I saw him progressing through college. He graduated from Indiana State University in Terre Haute, Indiana.

I was mad at myself that I couldn't and wanted that for myself. I wanted the best for everyone. His parents helped him throughout his college journey by supporting him financially and otherwise. When it came to my education and achievements in life, I did not have nobody.

Questioning God, I was like, "Why was I born? Why do I exist?" It really humbled me. God only knows the path for us. He knew us before the foundation of the world. My mother held me back from finishing college. I just needed help with financial aid, but she didn't want to help me.

I always asked her, "Can you help me get financial aid? I need your information so I can get financial aid. I'm not a legal adult as what the state looks at?" Her response was always a "no." I was mad at myself because of that. I wanted to progress through school at Ivy Tech. All I know is that the advisor met with me to inform me that my classes are being dropped because of the FAFSA. I knew why it had been dropped because I needed some information from my mother. As of today, I realized she *doesn't believe* in **education**.

That season made me feel so bad about

myself. Imagine not getting the help you need to better yourself. That season, I asked God, "Why can't I progress in school?" I wanted to further my education. The classes I was taking at the time I was going for nursing. I was looking up to one of my uncles, "Rees," who was in the medical field. He had been talking to me at the time a lot about my schooling.

He always said, "No excuses, nephew," every time I told him the situation. I used to get angry at myself because people didn't understand the situation. I wasn't making any excuses because I hated excuses myself. In the year of 2025, I told him the truth behind my struggle. I hate to complain but I will always give God the glory.

It's sad when your own people don't want you to do better than them. I considered myself a "Joseph" in my family. There are some individuals in my family who really hate the person I have become. Til this day, they try everything to bring me down.

When I got my BMW, I told my parents. One question I remember them asking me was, "Are you selling drugs? You are going to die." I just hung up the phone. Why would your parents be so cruel and think the worst? As a parent, you should want the best for your son or daughter–it's my opinion.

It doesn't make any sense when an individual gets blessed with something great, people think they are selling drugs. Selling drugs is not the only way to get amazing things and I am living proof. Drugs will have you locked up in prison or dead. I believe that if a man doesn't work, he doesn't eat. The things I have today, I am thankful for them, and I am humbled by it. You always have to have an occupied mind, to avoid a idle mind, the devil's workshop. An idle mind is the devil's playground (Proverbs 16:27-29).

Material things don't mean anything in this life. We can not take it with us when we leave earth. When I started providing for myself and working hard to get the things I have today, I reminisced on the days I didn't have a dime in my pocket. The nice clothes, shoes, housing, car, etc. that I have now, I still remain the person I was when I did not have anything to my name.

We as people can not make the materials on this earth our God. That is a no-no. God will snatch that thing away from you if you put something before him. We serve a jealous God. Put God first before anything.

The only thing we will leave this earth with is our character. So, how well did you treat people? How much did you love people like Christ loved us? We shouldn't put our all in cars, money, houses, people, sex, etc. The things on this earth are temporary. Keep your eyes on The Lord.

Proverbs 13:22 states, "**A good man leaveth an inheritance to his children's children.**" You may ask what the verse actually means. What's the breakdown of the verse? You have to leave something behind for your children's children. A life insurance policy is the main thing you can leave behind. Honestly, that is the only thing you can leave behind when dealing with finances.

As a young boy/young man, saving money for so many years was heavy on my mind. That was the only way, I thought, I could leave something behind. You cannot go wrong with investing money. I'm still trying to find avenues for investing my income. At the age of 28, I had gotten a life insurance policy for myself for under $40 a month.

Growing up, all I heard people talking about was a "GoFundMe" for funeral expenses. It's sad that there are individuals who are not educated on life insurance. I am guilty of learning about life insurance at a late age. Learning about life insurance should be taught in schools, as well as financial literacy, credit, how to invest income, and real estate, etc. Find a life insurance agent and get a quote that fits your budget from a reputable person. I recommend my Insurance agent, Yulanda Dyer, if you need help scan the QR or call her at 855-645-8255.

Yulanda Dyer

YulandaWholeLife.com

One day, I was talking to a relative about life insurance. People these days think life insurance is a scam after you educate them about it, though, they change their minds. I can't make them buy a policy, but only tell them, and pray God helps them with seeing the urgency and necessity. You have to leave something behind for your household. What legacy are you leaving behind for your household? You should consider this while you live and not just when death is certain. Check out "Your Legacy Moment" for how to build a legacy that you want to leave behind.

Your Legacy Moment

AuthorKLee.com

As of today, I have found out that the people who don't have life insurance policies for themselves used bank loans to cover the funeral expenses. You know those loans have high interest rates? Why pay $100 or more towards a bank loan when you can pay under $100 a month for a life insurance policy? The people who use "GoFundMe" to pay for funeral expenses don't get the money people contribute to the GoFundMe account right away, either. They have to wait for settlement and pay the fees they charge. So to make things easy, make sure your household is covered.

JACOB'S LADDER

BECOMING THE CHANGE I WANTED TO SEE

Jacob Bramlett

chapter

nine

Bad Company Corrupts Good Manners

1 CORINTHIANS 15:33

"Do not be deceived: "Bad company ruins good character."

In a world where I didn't look up to anyone, I created my path in life with God's direction. I always had this saying, "*There is no ladder set for me for where I am headed, so I'm climbing the ladder God gave me.*" There was no one I could look up to because of the environment I was surrounded by for years.

I thank God that I have not become what I was around and taught for years. Have you heard that you should be careful what you are around because that is what you will attract or become? Be cautious of the company you keep because "**Bad company corrupts good character" (1 Corinthians 15:33)**.

Yes, growing up as a child wasn't easy, but I thank God for the challenges. At the age of 12, I was diagnosed with Glaucoma. At the time, I did not know what glaucoma was. I remembered looking it up on the internet. All I saw was "blindness" on the internet. I started freaking out. I thought God punished me by giving me glaucoma.

Every night, I lost sleep thinking I was going to go blind. I was scared of losing my vision at that age. There were so many nights that I cried out to God in prayer. I asked God, "Can You touch my eyes, Lord?" I believed he was a healer. If you read John 9:1-41, you'll read about Jesus healing the blind man, and that was the verse I stood on for my healing.

As of today, I am still battling with Glaucoma. You know what's good about it? I am still claiming that I'm already healed. Sometimes you have to claim your healing over your mind, physically, and mentally. Remember that Jesus is a healer, and He is still healing in this season.

Back in 2018, at the age of 21, I remember the doctor asking me, "Do you have someone with you?" I responded, "No, I just got me, I don't have nobody to come to my doctor visits with me." The doctor responded, "I understand. I got some news to tell you." The doctor was telling me that I was losing sight in my left eye due to the disease. He showed me a diagram/report from the test. When I was told that, I started laughing in the room where the doctor and I were. All I saw on the report was nothing but black marks. The black marks on the reports symbolized "blindness."

The doctor looked at me crazily. He asked, "Are you ok, sir?" I remembered saying, "Jesus, going to take care of that. I don't have any worries, Doc." That moment messed with the doctor. I guess he had never seen anyone with crazy faith before. People have to realize, we do not serve a little God. We serve a big God.

I did my research on who had glaucoma in my family. I reached out to my elders and asked who they knew in our bloodline who had/have the disease. I was told that no one in our family ever had glaucoma. As of today, I can say God gave me that because God knows that I will overcome the disease. As of today, I'm still claiming my healing. Thank God that I am already healed. I am still believing that I will be healed once Jesus touches my eyes.

It was a day in the year of 2015, I went to my appointment to get my pressure checked. Every appointment, they dilated my eyes. The doctor responded, "I am so sorry, I have put the wrong eye drops in your eyes." I wanted to say something at the time to the doctor. At that moment, my eyes started to get heavy.

I couldn't see at the time. A lawsuit was on my mind as my eyes labored to readjust. Days later, while being home and going to school, I couldn't see for a week til the eye drops cleared out of my eyes. At the time, I thought the doctor had made me go blind by putting medication into my body. Some medications have different effects on individuals. Thank God I did not go blind on that day.

If I went blind, I would not know who would have taken care of me or who would be taking care of me besides God. God didn't see fit to allow that for me. He brought me through so much to the point that I just needed to have faith in him.

I can talk to anyone who is dealing with some type of sickness. I want to encourage you to know that we will claim our healing no matter what we see. God will not put you in a situation and/or circumstance just to leave you.

He's right there with you. Jesus is alive, and Jesus is still healing. Thank God that Jesus rose from the dead on the third day. Speak this over your life and your children's lives: "We are healed in Jesus' Name."

JACOB'S LADDER

BECOMING THE CHANGE I WANTED TO SEE

Jacob Bramlett

chapter

ten

My Heart had to Learn to Smile

PSALM 147:3

"He heals the brokenhearted and binds up their wounds."

So my great big sister, "Dr K Lee," and I started this book club called "The Growing Book Club" in January of 2025. The book club is amazing. So, it was an elder, "Power Gift" who asked me a question about it. The question was, "What advice would you give a young man who is dealing with mental health and abandonment issues?"

When that question was asked, I wasn't ready to respond right away because that was a question that I needed to do a sermon on. It was as if I were a preacher. I have a lot to say about the question.

I must admit I have struggled with my mental health for years. Thank God that it is better. I'm grateful I've experienced those moments, as I can now share with others how to navigate them. A person who's dealing with their mental health has to get close to God and have to be around people who love them. It was hard to find people who loved me while growing up. I always felt hated while growing up. I was the most hated, perhaps.

Abandonment issues? Yes, I had that while growing up. I was always isolated from everyone and from my siblings. I wasn't a problem child. I didn't cause any trouble or get any beatings with a belt or an extension cord. You may ask, "Why did you say extension cord?" From my experience, I have seen kids get beaten with extension cords. I was always separated from my other siblings.

I really wanted to have a good childhood with my siblings, but I couldn't because there was a different call on my life. As of today, I have one sister, "J'Leia." I treat her like she's my daughter. There are some folks who think she is my daughter when we go out together. We were born 21 years apart, and our birthdays are 1 day apart.

Some people need to stop having kids if they are not planning on being married or having help. If you are having kids from one-night stands, those "one-night stands" are the devil. That is a different subject. It is wild to have a sibling who wishes they were your child. A child is God's gift to a parent, that some day I would love to have.

My heart smiles when I know someone will have a bright future. All I know is God knows all, and he controls the future and the present. I pray for all the children and families born into families where they cannot flourish in education or are disconnected from their siblings. It can be lonely and brutally unfair.

All I know is that I wish I could talk to my younger self. What I would say is, "Jacob, I know that people don't like you because of your disability, the way you always stutter, the way you were always quiet. When you try to make friends, people always ignored you and made fun of you. Those same people will not prosper in life, continuing to do ugly to people. Be better than them and pray for them." In classrooms, I used to always have a desk in the corner. After all, I felt like my voice didn't matter because I always got cut off when I spoke as a kid.

Have you ever felt like you were misunderstood? I know I have as a kid, and especially as of today as an adult. God only knows, I have a bad habit of asking these phrases since I was a child: "You know what I mean?" and "You heard me?" I know the feeling of not being heard and always getting cut off. So you are not alone if you always get cut off when you speak. People still do it to me til this day.

At times, I told God that I would start wearing duct tape over my mouth since there are people who will always cut me off. For a year, I wore duct tape over my mouth when I went to gatherings, on a job, and even in the church. I would take it off to speak only to find I still got cut off, and I would put it back on. I thought to keep it off after that year, but I grew more frustrated with trying to communicate. It was normal for me to wear duct tape over my mouth, so I did it for an additional 3 years. My words didn't mean anything to anyone by how people treated and betrayed me.

The phrase "I Am" is the most powerful phrase. As it states in **Exodus 3:14, "I AM WHO I AM.**" God is I Am. We all have to be careful when we say phrases such as "I am stupid, dumb, etc." You are talking about God, too. Yes! Yes! We all have been there. As a kid, I remember telling God, "I am a retard like the guys told me at school. I am slow. Etc." I was talking about Him, too. We have to be very careful how we use the phrase **"I Am."**

Your thoughts can run your life. I am so guilty of experiencing that during my childhood years. Our thoughts can become our crime. Proverbs 4:23 states, **"Carefully guard your thoughts because they are the source of true life.**"

There is a saying, "The things I know now I wished I knew back then." We learn and grow each day that we see. You should start asking yourself, "What does God think of me?" He knows you by name. Just go run to him. He loves you.

On August 16, 2025, at 9pm, I got a word from God that I will be a preacher. Pastor Jacob's

Ladder sounds very deep when I think about it. God will put a gift within you to help others who are in need. God gave you a voice, so use the voice that you have to speak life over yourself and your children. God will do amazing things; you just have to believe it and trust God with all your heart.

Mental health is as important as your physical health. You have to protect your mental state daily. One thing that helps me with my mental health is going to the gym and listening to music. If I feel some type of way, I go to the gym or take a drive somewhere while the music is playing loudly in my car.

Back in 2019, I was in my apartment, all alone, in mental distress, with nobody to talk to. I called people —so-called "family," so-called friends, etc. —so I could just to talk to someone. I got so mad at myself that nobody wanted to talk to me. At the time, I couldn't call my parents because there was so much hatred against me.

That night, I called the police five times and then hung up. I didn't know that they were able to trace my address. They popped up at my place. I was so terrified hearing them knock at my door. As they knocked, I was under my bed, praying I wasn't in any real trouble. When I answered the door, they wouldn't stop knocking, and it sounded like it was getting louder. There were four cops dressed in uniform waiting for me at my door. I told the police to go away, because there was no emergency.

They didn't leave but insisted on coming in to

speak with me. They asked me if they needed to get an ambulance because they were concerned for me. It was nice to have someone to talk to and show concern, although I was embarrassed about the circumstances.

That night, I yelled at the police, "Why do people always ignore me? Why am I always getting cut off? Why do I feel like I am invisible to people?" The whole time, I was venting to them instead of God.

As a child, we moved to so many houses across Gary, Indiana, it was crazy. Stability wasn't as normal back then for me or anybody I knew. Every house and basement that we lived in, I started punching walls to the point that every home we had had holes in the wall throughout the entire house. I was so angry on the inside, heartbroken as a child, that I wanted to let out my pain in any way that I could.

As of today, it is hard for me to get angry at all. All the anger I had within me, I let it all out when I was a child. I do not remember a day when I wasn't angry as a child. It is pointless to get angry at certain things, I later learned. It is best to think things through and find the solution to the problem, then to punch holes in the walls.

I learned that I couldn't fix everything. When there was nothing that could be done, I just had to bite the bullet and keep pushing through as a child. When I spoke up as a child, I knew I would get told "shut up" because my words did not matter. The poor little boy I was, I should have been aborted because of how I was treated by others, I used to think.

Going to the shop or barbershop, all I can say is that there are great vibes there. They always make me feel at home and like someone who mattered. Being in the shop with my main AP and Twin, I can say it is nothing but therapy. Going to get haircuts at a young age wasn't a big possibility for me, but I love going to the shop every week or every 2 weeks at the most as an adult.

There are people who say, Don't cheat on your barber by going to another barber. Stick with your same barber. Why do you want to cheat on your barber or the person who does your hair? I like sticking to where I feel appreciated.

If there are any young men who dealt with what I dealt with, I just pull them aside and have a talk with them. I know how it feels when someone has no one to be vulnerable with. There was a day on my job back in 2019, when I was working with a coworker.

Me and this guy were talking about life. He told me he was stuck in life and depressed. I told him to give me an explanation why he feels stuck in life. He said that he feels down and heavy, and like he just couldn't move. There is some baggage and/or people that we are holding onto that we have to let go of to get where we want to go.

What is holding you bound? What baggage can you not let go of? Is the baggage you are holding onto **worth** holding? Start letting go of things that's not worth your peace. Put things in

God's hands and let God move through your life. You have to trust God with all of your heart.

The one thing that I learned in this life from my experience is so amazing. Think about this: if you rearrange the letters in "depression," you will get "I pressed on." Your current situation is not your final destination. Get up, dust yourself off, and keep pushing forward. There is nothing new under the sun that surprises God. He can handle your burdens, fears, problems, and questions.

JACOB'S LADDER

BECOMING THE CHANGE I WANTED TO SEE

Jacob Bramlett

chapter

eleven

I am Anointed by God

JOHN 14:1

"Don't be worried! Have faith in God and have faith in me."

Around the year of 2012, I was around the age of 15. At the time, I was still living in Gary, Indiana. By the middle of the year, I was relocated to East Chicago, Indiana. It was a city, and I didn't know anyone besides a couple of relatives. All I knew was that I couldn't go outside the house. At the time, I wasn't enrolled in school because I was taken out of school during my freshman year.

Have you felt like you were in a cage or a prison cell within your home? I have been in a cage for so long that I have learned how to adjust and get comfortable in the cage. When people come and try to tell me, "You are in a cage." I am all good because the last time I was out of the cage, it wasn't safe. The last time I trusted people, this is how they treated me. I was just going to hang in the cage.

The crazy part is I am anointed by God, but I am in the cage. I am called to own my own business, but I am in a cage. You can have everything in the cage but liberty (freedom). The cage offers you something that life doesn't offer you. The cage offers you a place that's always there.

Some of us are fearful of our own destiny, but we have to get to the point where we have faith in Jesus. As Jesus states in **John 14:1, "Don't be worried! Have faith in God and have faith in me."** You have to believe what he stated.

It was a statement my biological mother told me that I will never forget. It was one morning that I was going to walk to school because I did not have a ride to school. She once said, "You don't have to go back to school, you don't need a diploma." She really tried to keep me out of school. I started to get really angry at her and myself because she told me that. I really wanted to finish my freshman year of high school. I always thought education was important.

Why do parents not want their kids to have an education? Why do parents want to keep their kids illiterate? Why are parents abusing their kids emotionally and mentally? Education is free in this country, besides colleges and private schools.

Why would you turn down free education that can change your life? All I can say is, Jesus take the wheel. Let your will be done, Lord.

It does not make any sense that their parents want their kids to do badly in this life. What happened to the parents who want the best for their kids? It shouldn't be a new concept for kids to do better than their parents, right? I think differently, or I am strange compared to my parents. God bless you with a child to raise them the right way, not to lead them in the wrong direction. That's what the devil will do.

I really dislike my siblings' father; he was a good example of someone I didn't want to become. He showed me how to weigh white stuff, which I can say was "cocaine" now that I have lived more. He taught me how to put it in the little bags. At the time, I really felt so uncomfortable learning those things. I thought I was going to go to jail once I was exposed to it. It was at night that I was so paranoid because I thought the police were going to come after me.

My siblings' father started smoking the drugs heavily around me. I really hated the smell. On that day, he forced me to drink some alcohol that he had in a bottle. Once I drank it, I spit it out and threw the bottle across the room we were in. It was to the point that I called my grandmother, and told her about drugs being smoked around me. I told her to come get me. I had to sneak and call her.

During that day in the evening, I ran out the back door and ran away. I ran to an aunt's house out in East Chicago. It was about seven blocks away. I was scared and thought I was going to die because I ran away. I couldn't live under that roof anymore. My voice didn't matter under the roof. I was living but dead on the inside.

All I know is that my grandmother got in contact with my dad. He came and got me from where I was at. At the time, I still felt paranoid. It was plenty of nights, I never slept because I ran away. It was a time when I wanted to go back to that house to get the knives I slept with every night, and my belongings.

I knew I had to leave everything behind. At the time, I hated life and didn't want to live anymore. I thank God for helping me to run away and I trusted him to lead me to a better route. If I did not do what I did, I would not be in the position I am in today. I would be dead in the grave somewhere.

I had relocated to Chicago, Illinois, to be under my grandmother's wings. She took custody of me. I thank God that I have her in my life because she is truly a blessing to me. I just wish she could have raised all of her grandkids. Sadly, she only has a relationship with me out of all of her eleven grandchildren. I always asked God to have his love and protection over her life.

While in Chicago, Illinois, I felt like I was free from prison. I was so used to neglect and abuse. The teachings my grandmother gave me from the age of 15 til now, I appreciate the wisdom. While with her, I was still adapting to how I was living. I was worrying too much. My mind was all over the place. I felt like I was going to die. It felt weird because I wasn't sleeping with a knife. I felt naked because I didn't have a knife with me while sleeping.

It took me months to almost a year to start smiling. I thank God that I ran away. You may ask, "Why do you thank God you ran away?" I wouldn't have graduated from high school. I will be another statistic of the streets. I would not be telling my story.

I felt I was out of survival mode. I started thanking God every day that I can live. How many of us have ever been in survival mode? There can be times when we just live to get by each day. If you want to start living, be your authentic self and enjoy life. Tomorrow is not promised.

As of today, sometimes I wonder why my mother doesn't have a relationship with my grandmother (her mother). People are bitter and have hatred towards their own parents. It is sad that she teaches her kids to hate their grandmother. Let me keep my mouth closed. I don't have any business telling a parent what to do or anything like that. That is out of my roster.

I ask God to work on some people's hearts. Since she doesn't have a relationship with her mother, I came to the realization that I don't have a relationship with my own biological mother. What goes around comes around back to you. What seed are you producing? Do not be deceived. **God is not mocked, for whatever one sows, that will he also reap** (Galatians 6:7).

A parent has to be very careful how they

treat their seeds (their kids). What if your child told God that they wish they could choose their parents? How would you feel as a parent? I am 1000% guilty of asking God that question plenty of times for years. It is really sad that you do not feel any type of love from the person who gave birth to you. I never in my life heard the phrase, "I love you," from my mother. THAT IS SAD!!!!!

I always felt hated as a child. I always asked this question as a minor, "Where is the love for me?" There were plenty of days I begged people to love me, appreciate me, and acknowledge me. We have to embrace our crown as kings and queens.

There are people who tell me, "I will not have a woman because they are not for me." "Women do not want to have a conversation with you, Jacob." "You will never have a child in the future, Jacob," some said to me. The one that was the most discouraging, if I have a child in the future, my child will have so much hatred against me like my mother has towards her own mother."

If you heard something similar or thought it, I totally rebuke all of those sayings in the name of Jesus from your life and mine. Send it back to the sender from where it came from. The devil is a liar. If you have said this over your life, join me, denounce the things you said, and ask for the blood of Jesus to cover you, instead.

JACOB'S LADDER

BECOMING THE CHANGE I WANTED TO SEE

Jacob Bramlett

twelve

They Will Not Break Me

LUKE 6:37

"Who am I to judge another, when I myself walk imperfectly."

You may ask, are things in my past bothering me? I will be honest with you, in my early 20s, I was carrying so much baggage from the past for how people treated me. I was so hurt to the point that I couldn't trust anybody. At the time, I couldn't trust myself. I am proud of my heart. It's been played, stomped on, ripped apart, stabbed, cheated, burned, and broken, but somehow it still works. It was hard to find people who actually loved me.

I am the type of person who always forgives people. You have to forgive people for you. I don't believe in holding grudges. As of today, when people do me wrong, steal from me, retaliate against me, plot against me, etc. I just let things be. I don't believe in doing people how they do me. Vengeance is the Lord's.

There are people who try to break me down til this day. I keep my distance. Those individuals I still wish the best for, though. You may ask, "Why would you wish the best for people who try to break you?" What you wish upon others will come back on you sooner or later. I have been betrayed so much to the point that I am protective of my heart. I am cautious about who I let into my life and who I let close to me.

" **Who am I to judge another, when I myself walk imperfectly**" (**Luke 6:37**)? I don't believe in judging people. That is not my place to do. That is God's position to do that. There are people who think I am perfect. I do not want to be perfect. If an individual is perfect, how can they learn? Just really think about it. I have plenty of flaws and imperfections, but I embrace them. Start embracing your crown this day forward.

The last and only relationship I had in my life, I forgave the woman so many times to the point that she never had to apologize or own her mistakes. I was forgiving her constantly. You may ask, "Why didn't you just leave if she treated you poorly?" I hated being alone. In my next relationship, I know I want better, and I will have better for a wife and a mother of my children. I might not need ten or fifteen years; I am thinking five might be good enough. Will see.

My old point of view on women when I was hurting was, "I believed that women in my generation are the same." You may have told me, "They are not all the same, Jacob." And out of my pain, I would reply, "That's what I see. I see none but leeches and users."

When we are hurting, we can speak from our heart and penalize people who are not guilty of hurting us. Be careful of the words you speak about your feelings. When we are hurting, afraid, angry, or lonely, we can say things we don't mean or pray doesn't become our reality.

When I came to realize that I was alone in the most difficult times of my life, these times I noticed made me wiser, mature, and fearless. They strip away every illusion and show me who truly matters.

I learned that I had to become my own strength when no one showed up. In silence, I met the strongest version of myself. Pain was a great teacher and also experience on the way. The greatest teacher is love, more powerful than pain, regret, or shame. Growth will become your quiet reward. One day, you will look back and realize solitude was a blessing in disguise in the hands of God.

Things in this life were not handed to me. I had to get things out of the mud. I had to find the rose in the concrete and the silver lining to a bad script. Honestly, everything I have that is good, I know came from God. I thank God daily for the blessings I do have. I don't want to wait until things are gone before I know their value.

There have been seasons where I didn't hear from God. I wanted to question my direction because of the quietness. You want to know something that is very interesting: "The GPS on your phone or even in your car is silent when you are going in the right direction." You have to trust God through your process. God knows our lives, but we don't. God is Alpha and Omega (the beginning and the end).

In the next year or so, I'm looking forward to finding my wife out in Texas somewhere. Well, I will not be finding her. I got a word from God that she will find me. There's no rush getting into marriage. My 20s are all about self-discovery. When I was in my teens and early 20s, I always stated, "I will never have kids."

I stated that for one reason. That reason is, "You have to be very careful who you have a child with because it can mess your life up. Growing up, I thought I would never have a wife, so I could never have a child." What God has revealed to me, I want a child since I will have a wife in the future. I want a daughter. If I have a son, he will be a junior, and I will be equally grateful.

I know I will be a great father to my household. Parenting isn't easy at all. Being a parent, though, is truly a blessing. While I am seeing how people parent their kids, I see so much that I can change within that. When it comes to parenting, it will never be perfect.

Parenting is a process, and it is also a journey. First thing, there is one verse I live by, it is coming from Proverbs 22:6. It states, "**You have to train up a child the way he should go; when he is old, he will not depart from it.**" What are you teaching your kids? What are you instilling within them? Are you teaching them about God, education, the meaning of life, etc?

As a father in the future, I will tell my daughter or son how I was raised up and how I was treated. I will never let my child experience any mental and emotional abuse. Growing up, I wasn't raised in a home with praying parents. This is different than what will happen in the household I will have with my wife; she will know she will have a praying husband. My children will know they got a praying daddy.

A father must pray, as a mother should. Fathering is a ministry, as well as mothering. As a parent, *I do not want to see my child fail like my parents did me. In this life, a child may have to experience some things. BUT, **not all** things are necessary to happen.*

As a father, I want the best for my child. What will be instilled within my daughter or son is what I wanted to be instilled within me as a child. "This is the ladder I am building to connect to my future. This is me becoming the change I wanted to see!" I totally believe having a child is part of my healing my heart from all of the emotional and mental abuse I have experienced in my lifetime.

As a father, if my child messes up on something or makes a mistake, I will show her or him where they made the mistake and how to

correct it. I would not say, "I told you so." Let your
child learn without your extra. This is one truth:
some kids have to bump their heads to learn.
As a child, I did not have the proper guidance,
so I had to learn based on my experiences. You
have to wait a while before you say, "A hard head
makes a soft behind."

JACOB'S LADDER

BECOMING THE CHANGE I WANTED TO SEE

Jacob Bramlett

thirteen

God Knows What You Need

MATTHEW 6:7-8

"And when you pray, do not heap up empty phrases as the Gentiles do, for they think that they will be heard for their many words. 8 Do not be like them, for your Father knows what you need before you ask him."

Friends? I used to dislike that term until God blessed me with an individual who I called my big sister, "Dr. K Lee." She's one of the greatest people I have in my life. By the way, she has published 52 books as of today, and she still working to be over a hundred original titles! It's tough trying to find good people in this world. Thank God for good people.

Author K Lee

AuthorKLee.com

I still communicate with some of the guys I went to college with at Philander Smith College, which is now a university. "The P" will always be home. A couple of people I can name: LaKendrick, Paytre, a couple of sets of twins, Tarai and Jalan, Spark and Aminah, and Darnell and Chet. These are some of my friends I talk to from time to time on social media. I can say that they are some good people doing great things.

I wished my parent had given me what I needed for financial aid because I would have had a bachelor's degree under my belt from Philander Smith College. During that time period, I was also homesick. The people I came from didn't want me to progress in life because of the jealousy they have in their spirit. I am still thankful that I have a degree/certification in early childhood development under my belt. Sometimes, you have to thank God for the small things.

God only knows who will enter and leave our lives. People are either a lesson or a blessing. On July 27, 2022, I met a queen on the job. My eyes got big when I saw this individual. All I know is that I told God I was going to approach the woman. When she told me her name, all I knew was that I felt heaven around her. Her name spells Heaven backwards.

I totally believed that I was on an assignment to help her throughout her last 2-3 years of college at Ball State. I thank God that I had the opportunity to help, support, and encourage her to get her bachelor's degree. As a friend, I believe that you have to look out for one another. She will be in my prayers daily for the loss of her dad. I really appreciate the conversations we have once a month.

We have to accept the fact that you may be placed in people's lives to help them for a season. Being a good person with a great heart and pure intentions really will make you feel like you are being used all the time by God. It was my assignment to help Nevaeh to get through her last years of undergrad, not being cocky or anything about that matter. I truly thank God that she got her degree! I truly thank God that I was able to help her. She deserves that "big degree."

If you ask God to use you, sometimes we will get assignments from God that do not benefit us directly at the moment. That is a hard pill to swallow. I felt that God was shining through me to help individuals. I remember telling God that I wished I had someone like me in my life when I needed help. I guess this is another example of me being the change I wanted to see!

Back in 2017, I met this woman in a large

retail store. I wasn't comfortable making friends because my trust was so messed up that I couldn't trust anyone. I stepped out of my comfort zone, and I approached a dark skinned woman. We ate lunch together that I bought us, and we even laughed. I thought we had a good vibe going on. I remember we had a bad winter storm. I wasn't comfortable walking in it because I was catching the city buses to get where I needed to go, and I did not know how to drive. I didn't have my license or a car at the time. She started giving me rides every day that I worked.

I thought God blessed me with a great friend. Weeks later, we started to get to know each other. She was 20 at the time, and I was 22. I thought that wasn't a big age difference to be good friends. Back then, we used to always have the same shift together at work. So we went to work together and left work together. This wasn't a relationship thing but a friendship or co-working convenience.

After a month of knowing each other, she stated that she had 10 kids. I responded, "That's ok, I understand, I'll be there for the kids, if the father is not around." She had 7 boys and 3 girls. She had 5 baby fathers. She had a set of 5 twins. As of today, with the mindset I have now, I should have run from that friendship!!!!!!!!!!!!!!!!!! I could only imagine how my life would be if I got trapped in a relationship!

There were days I babysat her kids. I can say what an experience, Me and the boys got along very well. I enjoyed hanging out with them, taking them to the movies, and buying them shoes. I was paying a lot of money because I wanted to help and show my care. All of my money was going to the kids instead of my responsibilities. I was neglecting myself and my responsibilities. I should have talked to God when I was meeting someone new. The things I know now, I wished I knew back then!

This friendship really traumatized me. I felt like I was in prison. It was one night, I had her and her kids living with me because she didn't have a place to stay. She was really angry at me for some reason. She quit her job, so she was depending on me to take care of her and her kids. I paid her car note and her insurance each month. I was working endless hours to the point that I didn't have time for myself or any goals I wanted to accomplish.

Months later, I was drained to the point that I couldn't move on in life. During that era, I wasn't in Church because I did not have a Church home. I always stayed in God's word, though. I started questioning God about the circumstances I was in. I could not blame God; I had to take self-accountability for my actions, you know? First, I didn't talk to God before meeting this individual. Second, I was being thirsty by choosing anyone to be my friend and not choosing a woman who valued marriage, children, and raising a family like how I wanted to.

While me and this woman lived with each other, she was depending on food stamps each month. She didn't believe a woman should work, just the man. It was months since she brought groceries into the house. One statement that she once said was, "You can not eat any of the food that I will bring into this house. The food is just for me and my kids." I remember days I had to sneak to eat food in my own crib that I paid rent and bills for each month.

The old me was rising above the situation and was telling myself, "It's all good." For many nights, I was so paranoid. It was hard for me to sleep. There were nights I slept on the patio. I can state that it was a night, I was sleeping peacefully in my bed, and all I knew was that a gun was in my face.

The woman had a gun in my face, ya'll!!!!!! I started to freak out. I thought I was going to die. All I was told was, "Do not move before I shoot your face off. I want to do witchcraft on you." My mind was all over the place. I could not breathe. I did not know what to do. I felt the enemy, satan, was in my room.

She started talking to herself while the gun was in my face, towards my eyes. The fear I had within me, I was lost for words. If I moved or said a word, I knew she would shoot me instantly. She said, "This gun is cock and loaded, I will shoot you. Do not play with me." Have you felt like the devil was next to you? Looking you in your eyes???? I know I have.

There were times she stole all of my money in my savings, stole my identity, got a hold of my social security number, used my credit for things I didn't know about, etc. She got personal loans under my name, and got 3 late payments on my credit profile. I was so overwhelmed with life. One statement she said was, "If you ever leave me, you will die, so do not leave." At that point, I did not know what to do or who to talk to.

No one talked to me from the beginning about leaving that friendship. Folks did not care about my well-being or my life. I was a big burden to folks. If I could turn back the hands of time, I would just stay to myself and be a loner as I am as an adult.

That season of my life had me questioning God. I was experiencing domestic violence within the friendship. It was a saying she always said that creeped me out. "I'm the devil. Don't mess with me." That woman would beat me out of my sleep at 2 o'clock in the morning. I knew I couldn't hit a woman because a man shouldn't put his hands on a woman.

I called the police. When the police came, I told the officers, "Get the woman out of my apartment unit." She didn't want to leave because she and her kids did not have anywhere to go. The woman stated, "Get Jacob out of the apartment before I kill him." The police told me to leave the apartment where I paid rent.

I refused to leave my apartment. It was not right for the person who was on the lease to leave. During that moment, I did not leave the apartment. I just sat on the floor. The police hit me with the taser and dragged me from my legs out of my apartment and told me I had to go.

I called people for some advice on the situation, but there was no answer. Some people answered my call and told me to just figure it out on my own. I walked 3 hours to my job and just slept at my job for a week. I know I couldn't go back to the home I paid rent at.

I stopped paying rent at the apartment. I made the decision not to pay rent because I did not want to pay if I'm not living there. I was expecting to get evicted because of the decision I made. That decision fell on me the hardest. I know I had to take self-accountability for my decisions. I couldn't blame it on anyone but myself.

That friendship really changed how I looked at things. She always wonders why her kids loved being around me. She once asked me, "Why do my kids always want to be around you and talk to you? Why are they so happy around you? What did you do to my kids?" I told her, "Talk to your kids. I will not speak for them. They can speak for themselves since they can talk."

They always asked about me when I met them. It's amazing when a kid loves your presence. I treat all kids like they are my kids. That's coming from my heart. My heart is too big. There are times that I have to protect my heart because this heart of mine got stomped on and ripped apart. My heart was broken, stolen, and busted wide open. I felt like my heart could not be fixed because it was broken into pieces constantly.

Somewhere in your journey, there will be an "**unsaved**" person who does the things that will be done, and you remain blameless. She thought to take advantage of me, but her children were innocent. Sad to say this, everybody isn't going to Heaven. Everybody isn't Christian or loves God. There are some people who will reject The Lord.

The things I know now, I wish I knew back then. I would've called a relative of mine back in Gary, and handled what needed to be handled. I would have told her the situation and told her to do what she needed to do to help me get this woman out of my apartment. There are family members we all have that are not shy about doing our dirty work. The people who know how to make unmovable people move. You don't ask questions; you just appreciate their help.

The trauma I had from that friendship, I just do not have words for. I thought I could not heal from that chapter of my life because of how broken my heart was. I give God the glory for healing me, protecting me, and delivering me from that chapter of my life. It took 5 years to heal from that trauma. My God!

It is more dangerous to have fear of people than God. The friend I thought I had put some fear in my heart. It was either I was going to die in the friendship or walk away. She wasn't the only one who took advantage of my kindness; it was also family. I always thought a parent could be your best friend. Well, I should have thought differently. I gave my parent everything I had financially. The old me thought that was a good thing to do when it comes to obeying your parents.

It was a time when the household was short on bills, no food in the house, etc. So I was thinking about how to help with things. I gave everything I had in my savings, which was $2,000, and I applied for a personal loan for $2,100. I thought that was enough to help out the household. To cover bills and to make sure my siblings were taken care of.

The whole time, I didn't have any cushion to fall back on when I had an emergency. When it came to the personal loan. I wasn't educated on interest rates at the age of 24. You may ask why not? I was living life just to get by. I had no one helping me to learn about finances; everything I learned was by firsthand experience because people did not like talking to me.

The interest rate on the personal loan was 138%. **THAT IS NOTHING BUT FINANCIAL HOMICIDE RIGHT THERE!!** There was a 24-month term for a certain amount I had to pay each month. I was wondering why this loan keeps adding dollars to the principal? I was getting frustrated to the point that I worked endless hours to save up the money and pay the loan off in full. The family member I did it for did not want to help me pay it off. The whole time, I was forced to apply for the loan because their problems now became my problem.

I was so mad at myself. All of that gave me a lesson on things. I stopped being so kind to individuals. I don't trust the people that I came from. During that moment, I felt I could only trust God. Have you blamed God for the situations that you had to deal with? Well, I didn't blame God; I hold myself accountable for the decisions I made.

chapter thirteen: God Knows What You Need

Money? Money? Money? People like that term until they have to work for it. Right? I am guilty of buying friendships and the relationship I had. It was normal for me to pay $100 to $200 a week for relationships and even some friendships. The realization of it all was that I was being used. Now you see how I can think people who are my age, family, and friends are users and leeches. The truth is, I didn't have good company, I found out later.

During this era of my life, buying friendships came to an end with me. I had had enough of being used. Thank God I know my worth. If there were a way I could get a W2 from the friendships and family members I bought items for or paid money to have them in my life, I could be in another tax bracket! Shame we don't get W2s for that.

Every friendship that I thought I had, the trust was broken. There was a saying, "Everybody is not your friend." As a kid, my mother also had me isolated, and once she told me, "You don't need any friends. Nobody wants to be around you." Then I went somewhere in the basement or a room and just learned to be comfortable in the isolation I was in.

Everyone has a Judas in their life. It could be a relative, a friend, a sibling, or it can be your own parent. There is always a Judas in the crowd. It was a season in my life that the Judas in my life was exposed. It was really painful to find out who the Judas was in my life. I was lost for words. I honestly think I had more than one Judas!

My Lord Jesus was betrayed by one of his disciples, Judas. He agreed to betray Jesus in the book of Matthew, Chapter 26, verses 14 to 16, which reads: **"Judas Iscariot was one of the twelve disciples. He went to the chief priests and asked, "How much will you give me if I help you arrest Jesus?" They paid Judas 30 silver coins, and from then on, he started looking for a good chance to betray Jesus**."

A friendship can be a cave if it is not genuine. God let me have the friendships I had, in which I don't have any more to humble me. I was in a cave. You want to know something?

God will put you in a cave to humble you. God will use the cave to speak to you. Great victories can lead to great unexpected trials.

JACOB'S LADDER

BECOMING THE CHANGE I WANTED TO SEE

Jacob Bramlett

chapter

fourteen

Turning Back the Hands of Time

JOHN 3:16

"For God so loved the world, that he gave his only begotten Son, that whosoever believeth in him should not perish but have everlasting life."

I know the last chapter was hard, even filled with terrible events. But this story gets better because I know the author personally. There are better days ahead when you keep your eyes on the Lord. I do not care how dark your past was; you can still become light. I remembered I needed therapy, but didn't have the funds for a consultation.

Where would I be without my struggle?

Where would I be without my pain? It hurts me some days when my parents do not want a relationship with me. But I had to learn "who is my mother or father, except those who are in Christ?" I had to accept the parents he gave me, not just the ones I was born to. He has used many people in my life to mother and father me over the years.

When I keep my eyes on the Lord, life is worth living. Back in my high school years from 2013 to 2015, I was a teacher's assistant at Bethune Preschool in Gary, Indiana. The passion I had and still have for children is amazing. I love working with kids and teaching kids. It felt like I was the main teacher of the class.

Only if I could turn back the hands of time when I was in the school teaching the babies. Back then, when I was in the teaching field, the kids called me "Mr. Jacob or Mr. J". I was ok with being called that because they did not know how to pronounce my last name. It was days when as a teacher, I helped with putting children on the bus to go home. There were some children who did not want to leave because they wanted me to be right with them.

That made my heart smile each day while I was working with the kids. There is a girl named Jasmine and a boy named Cleo who I taught, who are now 14 years old. They were born nine months apart. Their mom found me on social media and asked me if I remembered her children when they attended Bethune Preschool?

The parent said to me online, "They have

been asking about you for a long time. It's amazing how you made a big impact on my kids. Thank you for what you have instilled within my children." I believe it takes a village to raise a child. You train a child the way they should go.

While working in the preschool, I remember teaching lessons to the children. I made the teaching fun. It was a day that will never be forgotten, when me and the class were learning about the types of animals there are. One of the children asked me, "Are you a gorilla?" I just started laughing to the point tears came down my face. I responded, "No, but I can show you what one looks like." I learned that even little children had some jokes about me.

When it came to field trips each year, I was a chaperon. We all went on field trips. In the Fall, we went to the zoo and the apple orchard. Back then, I felt like my dreams had come to reality. The passion I had while working with children was remarkable.

Working with kids is my happy place. People may state, "They cannot tell, because I have been in retail for so many years." I tried to get jobs in schools, but the pay rate that they were offering me wasn't in my range to live on. I totally believe that money isn't everything, but we all need money to live and support ourselves.

I consider myself a big brother or uncle to children. I actually love mentoring young people. When I see young children, I ask myself what can I tell them that I wish I knew at their age. I totally understand that some children don't have guidance in their homes or some children don't have anyone they can look up to or be vulnerable with.

In my high school years, I will never forget. I fought the same big dude throughout my high school years for bullying me. He was 6 '5 while I was 5' 1 at the time. I wasn't afraid to fight Goliath like how David wasn't afraid to fight him either.

I was ready to fight that dude in school for bullying me and everything he had done to me. People were so jealous of me because I was the biggest flirt in the school. I was always beside a girl in the hallways and even in classrooms. The whole entire time, I was getting played. I was just following along. After 4 years of flirting with girls at the school, I was rewarded for being the biggest flirt in the school at our senior luncheon.

I was also rewarded for being the most responsible individual and having the best smile. I made sure I was on top of my work. In the end, I graduated at the top of my class with "National Honor Society" with a 3.9 GPA, and I was accepted to 13 universities, with so many scholarships. In all the schools I applied for, I got a full ride; everything was all paid for!

Yes, the guy who was several grades behind in learning caught up and got the highest position. The best way to respond to trouble is to win despite it.

During the Summer of 2025 me, my nieces and nephews, had a blast. Since I barely had a childhood, I don't hesitate to relive the moments

I missed and just be a big kid having fun. I was acting like my shoe size, playing with them in the ball pit, going down slides, and building with them. You may think that is wild. Hey, I say, "Live life, tomorrow is not promised. Be thankful for each day God gave you."

One day, my niece Zoe asked me, "Why are people so mean to you? That makes me sad," I had to explain to her that they are just showing their true colors of their character." People are going to be who they are. The best response to some situations is silence. Silence can make a powerful noise.

In my life, I get along well with older adults. You may ask, why? The mentality that I have is above most people my age. I had to become responsible young, so I have the maturity of an older adult because of my experiences. I am twice my age mentally.

I truly thank God that I didn't become what was instilled in me. I could be out here selling dope, be in gangs, sleeping with a lot of women, or be in prison doing some time. You have to make the decision to become what you have been taught or move in a different direction. Getting everything out of the mud was not easy, but I appreciate the things I work for by the direction of God.

The honest truth that is hard to accept is that there is nothing I can take from my biological parents into this life. They are people I do not want to be like. I do not want a woman like my mother, and I will not be a father like my dad. I believe in being better than your parents. The cycle ends with me.

Even if it makes the people I came from uncomfortable. I can only give thanks to God for elevating me and continuing to raise up the ladder that I am climbing in this life. I am not better than no one. I'm better than who I was yesterday. The only person I will compare myself to is the person I was yesterday.

If you want to be better than you were yesterday and you have not given your life to Christ, I want to invite you to a prayer of salvation. This prayer will invite the Father into your life as your Helper, Friend, Father, Savior, and Redeemer. If you know you need to overcome life challenges, then please join me in this prayer.

Salvation Prayer:

"Dear God, thank you for sending your Son, Jesus Christ, to die for my sins. Thank you for giving me a way of escape from all my troubles. I believe that Jesus is your Son. I believe that Jesus has died and rose on the third day. Without Jesus, I will not be with you; I will be in death because I am a sinner. I can not get to you on my own. I believe that Jesus is your Son. I believe Jesus is the only way to you. Jesus states, " I am the way and the truth and the life." I believe that Jesus had risen from the dead after 3 days. Thank you, God, that Jesus is alive. Thank you, God, for your Son, Jesus. In Jesus' Name Amen."

Scriptures That Will Encourage You

- ### Genesis 28:10-22

Jacob left the town of Beersheba and started out for Haran. At sunset, he stopped for the night and went to sleep, resting his head on a large rock. In a dream, he saw a ladder that reached from earth to heaven, and God's angels were going up and down on it. The Lord was standing beside the ladder and said: I am the Lord God who was worshiped by Abraham and Isaac. I will give you and your family the land on which you are now sleeping. Your descendants will spread over the earth in all directions and will become as numerous as the specks of dust.

Your family will be a blessing to all people. Wherever you go, I will watch over you, then later I will bring you back to this land. I won't leave you–I will do all I promised. Jacob woke up early the next morning, he took the rock that he had used for a pillow and stood it up as a place of worship. Then he poured olive oil on the rock to dedicate it to God, and he named the place Bethel.

Before that, it had been named Luz. Jacob solemnly promised God, "If you go with me and watch over me as I travel, and if you give me food and clothes and bring me safely home again, you will be my God. This rock will be your house, and I will give back to you a tenth of everything you give me.

- **James 1:2-3**

My brethren, count it all joy when ye fall into divers temptations; knowing this, this, that the trying of your faith worketh patience.

- **John 3:16**

For God so loved the world, that he gave his only begotten Son, that whosoever believeth in him should not perish but have everlasting life.

- **Numbers 14:28**

Say unto them. As truly as I live, saith the Lord, as ye have spoken in my ears, so will I do to you.

- **Joshua 1:9**

Have I commanded thee? Be strong and of good courage; be not afraid, neither be thou dismayed: for the Lord thy God is with thee whithersoever thou goest.

- **Exodus 14:14**

The Lord will fight for you, and you won't have to do a thing.

- **Isaiah 41:10**

Don't be afraid, I am with you. Don't tremble. With fear. I am your God. I will make you strong, as I protect you with my arm.

- **Isaiah 43:19**

I am creating something new. There it is! Do you see it? I have put roads in deserts, streams in thirsty lands.

- **Psalm 28:7**

The Lord is my strength and my shield; my heart trusted in him, and I am helped: therefore my heart greatly rejoiceth; and with my song will I praise him.

- **Ecclesiastes 3:11**

He hath made every thing beautiful in his time: also he hath set the world in their heart, so that no man can find out the work that God maketh from the beginning to the end.

- **Psalm 91**

The Lord Is My Fortress

Live under the protection of God Most High and stay in the shadow of God All-Powerful. Then you will say to the Lord, "You are my fortress, my place of safety; you are my God, and I trust you." The Lord will keep you safe from secret traps and deadly diseases. He will spread his wings over you and keep you secure. His faithfulness is like a shield or a city wall. You won't need to worry about dangers at night or arrows during the day. And you won't fear diseases that strike in the dark or sudden disaster at noon. You will not be harmed, though thousands fall all around you.

And with your own eyes you will see the punishment of the wicked. The Lord Most High is your fortress. Run to him for safety, and no terrible disasters will strike you or your home. God will command his angels to protect you wherever you go. They will carry you in their arms, and you won't hurt your feet on the stones. You will overpower the strongest lions and the most deadly snakes.

The Lord says, "If you love me and truly know who I am, I will rescue you and keep you safe. When you are in trouble, call out to me. I will answer and be there to protect and honor you. You will live a long life and see my saving power.

● Psalm 54

Save me, God, by your power and prove I am right. Listen to my prayer and hear what I say. Cruel strangers have attacked and want me dead. Not one of them cares about you. You will help me, Lord God, and keep me from falling; you will punish my enemies for their evil deeds.

Be my faithful friend and destroy them. I will bring a gift and offer a sacrifice to you, Lord. I will praise your name because you are good. You have rescued me from all my troubles, and my own eyes have seen my enemies fall.

● Hebrews 11:1

Now faith is the substance of things hoped for, the evidence of things not seen.

● Philippians 4:6

Be careful for nothing; but in every thing by prayer and supplication with thanksgiving let your requests be made known unto God.

● Acts 2:24

But God set him free from death and raised him to life. Death could not hold him in its power.

- **Micah 7:7**

But I trust the Lord God to save me, and I will wait for him to answer my prayer.

- **2 Peter 1:3**

We have everything we need to live a life that pleases God. It was all given to us by God's own power when we learned he had invited us to share in his wonderful goodness.

- **Psalm 56:8**

You have kept a record of my days of wandering. You have stored my tears in your bottle and counted each of them.

- **Colossians 4:6**

Be pleasant and hold their interest when you speak the message. Choose your words carefully and be ready to give answers to anyone who asks questions.

- **Malachi 3:7**

Even from the days of your fathers ye are gone away from mine ordinances, and have not kept them. Return unto me, and I will return unto you, saith the Lord of hosts. But ye said, Wherein shall we return?

- **John 3:16**

For God so loved the world, that he gave his only begotten Son, that whosoever believeth in him should not perish but have everlasting life.

- **Habakkuk 2:3**

At this time, I have decided that my words

will come true. You can trust what I say about the future. It may take a long time, but keep on waiting– it will happen.

- **Joshua 1:9**

I've commanded you to be strong and brave. Don't ever be afraid or discouraged! I am your Lord, your God, and I will be there to help you wherever you go.

- **John 14:1**

Jesus said to his disciples, "Don't be worried! Have faith in God and have faith in me.

JESUS IS THE WAY TO THE FATHER!!!!

JACOB'S LADDER

BECOMING THE CHANGE I WANTED TO SEE

Jacob Bramlett

about the

author

Jacob Bramlett

Jacob's Ladder is all about progressing. In this life, I totally believe that life is a journey. God places people in my life for a season or a lifetime. No matter what I faced in the past, I'm always looking forward to the future. All the homes I lived in with people I barely knew throughout my childhood really built the man I am today.

I believe education is important. I'm furthering my education by the grace of God. God is first in everything that I do. I'm reaching the top of the ladder. What's on top could be a bigger blessing than what I expect it to be.

No matter how people treated me, abandoned me, etc. that will not change the person I am today. I just had to bite the bullet when I was going through my seasons. I do not believe in doing bad things to people. I am not perfect, but I did some things that I have regretted.

Do I wish my story could be better? No! If the things that happened in my life did not happen,

I would not be the person I am today. I could not become the change I wanted to see!

There are more books in my future, and this is the first of many.

about the author: Jacob Bramlett

SCAN ME

Call or Text:
770-240-0089 Press Extension 1
Web: KLEpub.com
Email Services@klepub.com

It's time to start and finish   **YOUR Story**!

KLE Publishing specializes in helping people become authors. In as little as 15 to 90 days, we can help you develop your books and e-books and publish to 39,000 outlets! We also offer audiobook services.

Write, Edit, Format, Publish
We can help from
Start to Finish.

Explore and learn more about published authors affiliated with KLE.

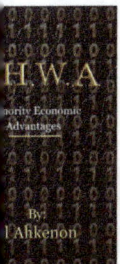

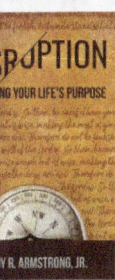

KLEPub.com